SEATTLE'S
FORGOTTEN
SERIAL
KILLER

GARY GENE GRANT

CLOYD STEIGER

THE
History
PRESS

Published by The History Press
Charleston, SC
www.historypress.com

First published 2020

Manufactured in the United States

ISBN 9781467143622

Library of Congress Control Number: 2019951255

When I close my eyes, I can see all these things happening,
like I were a movie camera…

—Gary Gene Grant psychiatric evaluation, June 1971

CONTENTS

ACKNOWLEDGEMENTS

When I was asked to write this book, I looked for people directly involved in the case who could help me fill in the blanks the case file could not. I quickly found that many of the people who worked on, prosecuted or were affected by the Gary Grant case had passed away.

I reached out to current Renton mayor Denis Law, who put me in contact with the Renton Historical Society and its curator, Dr. Elizabeth Stewart. She was very helpful in giving me not only information about this case but also other historical facts about Renton.

Renton councilmember and retired Renton police assistant chief Don Persson gave me great insight into the Renton Police Department during those times. He also linked me to John Pavone, who had been a detective with the police department and worked on the Grant case.

Jim Phelan was gracious in sharing his memories of the investigation, including insights that didn't come out in the official case file.

Wally Hume, who had a significant role in the case, also told me what he remembered, after saying, "I've spent years and years trying to forget this case…" but still having the inside information I was looking for.

Elected King County prosecutor Christopher Bayley was instrumental in relaying his thoughts about this notorious case that came to light just weeks after he took office.

Although Special Prosecutor Edmund Allen had passed away just a year before I started this project, his son, Edmund Allen Jr., himself an attorney and former King County prosecutor, was very helpful in describing the conversations he had with his father about this incident and how deeply affected the elder Allen was by the case.

Michael DiJulio and I crossed paths many times when I worked as a homicide detective and he as a longtime prosecutor. His insights into the case were equally invaluable.

Casey McNerthney is a friend and longtime reporter/executive producer in the Seattle news market who helped me with research and gave me useful contacts to complete this book.

Lastly, I can't write this book without acknowledging the anguish suffered by the friends and families of Carol Erickson, Joanne Zulauf, Scott Andrews and Bradley Lyons. Their suffering is that of often-overlooked secondary victims of homicide: the loved ones left behind.

INTRODUCTION

Throughout the years, people have been fascinated by serial killers. From the Whitechapel murders of Jack the Ripper to the more modern John Wayne Gacy, Ted Bundy, Wayne Williams (the Atlanta Child Murderer) and Gary Ridgway (the Green River Killer), these cases have demanded the attention of the masses with various books, documentaries and articles written about the incidents. Although these killers account for a scintilla of the murders committed in the United States, criminologists have committed their academic lives to the study of these human enigmas to see what makes them tick.

In this age of vast information resources, most of these killers are well known to the students of this type of crime. Volumes have been written about them and are only a mouse-click away for anyone interested in researching them. Many serial killers' names are well known to those who study them, either as a hobbyist or an academic. People are often surprised to learn that the vast majority of serial killers are not generally known by the public.

Even though I was a longtime homicide detective who worked on serial murder cases and studied many others, there are known serial killers who I've never heard of. To have one who operated in the Seattle area who I hadn't heard of was surprising; I thought I knew most of the local suspects.

A year before I wrote this book, I received an e-mail from someone who had read my first book, *Homicide: The View from Inside the Yellow Tape*: "What do you know about Gary Grant, who killed two teenaged girls and two small boys in Renton in the late sixties or early seventies?"

Though I thought I knew about most if not all of the serial killers in Washington State, I had never heard of Grant. Inquiries to the Renton Police Department and King County Sheriff's Office revealed only a small, incomplete footprint of the crime.

When I contacted the King County Prosecutor's Office, it had the court file for the case and allowed me to copy it for submission to the Homicide Investigations Tracking Systems database where I currently work.

Later, when The History Press asked if I would write a historical true crime book from the Seattle area, this case immediately came to mind.

Besides poring over the case file, I tried to find people who were associated with this case. Many had passed away. I was able to find some, like Detectives Wally Hume and John Pavone, as well as then-sergeant Jim Phelan, who had personally worked on the case. Don Perrson was an officer and later assistant chief and Renton City Council member and discussed with me the Renton Police Department at the time and how this case affected the city and the department.

Edmund Allen, who was appointed as special prosecutor for this case, had passed away the year before I began working on this book, but his son, attorney Edmund Allen Jr., related some of the many conversations he had with his father over the years about the Grant case.

Former elected King County prosecutor Christopher Bayley shared his memories of the case, some of which he detailed in his book, *Seattle Justice: The Rise and Fall of the Police Payoff System in Seattle*. Michael DiJulio, who prosecuted this case with Allen, shared his insights.

Judge David Soukup, who presided over *State v. Gary Gene Grant*, was still around; I spoke to him about the case and how his rulings kept Grant from walking free after serious errors by a member of the Renton Police Department.

Slowly, the case emerged for me. Speaking with those still around who worked the case, I learned that they still had fresh memories of it. It had made an indelible mark on their collective minds.

With the benefit of twenty-twenty hindsight, I learned about the case, about mistakes made and the excellent detective work done by investigators with little or no experience in working on a crime of this magnitude—without all the modern forensic tools available today.

And I learned about Gary Gene Grant: Seattle's forgotten serial killer.

CAROL

December 1969 was a turbulent time in America. Richard Nixon was finishing his first year in the presidency while protests filled the streets of major cities across the country because of the Vietnam War.

"Leaving on a Jet Plane" by Peter, Paul and Mary topped the charts, along with "Na Na, Hey Hey, Kiss Him Goodbye" by Steam and "Sugar, Sugar" by the Archies. At the movies, the James Bond film *On Her Majesty's Secret Service* lit up the screen, along with *Cactus Flower*, starring Goldie Hawn, and *Hello, Dolly!* featuring Barbra Streisand and Walter Matthau.

Americans celebrated Apollo 11's auspicious moon landing the previous summer while being shocked by the murders committed in Los Angeles by the Charles Manson cult. This was a few years before Ted Bundy stalked women in the local area. The term "serial killer" was not yet in the American vocabulary.

Renton, Washington, which would boast a population of almost 100,000 in 2019, was a small town of about 18,000 in 1969, situated about eleven miles southeast of downtown Seattle, at the south end of Lake Washington. Its major employer was the Boeing plant in town, which churned out the B-29 Superfortress during World War II before converting to the production of 707s in the late '50s. Its most famous resident is Jimi Hendrix, who is buried on a hill east of downtown.

The Cedar River meanders through the sleepy burg before dumping into Lake Washington, its banks often lined with anglers hoping to pull in a steelhead trout or a migrating salmon.

Left: Renton, Washington's most famous resident, Jimi Hendrix, is buried in the Renton Highlands, just a few blocks from Renton Vocational School, where both Carol Erickson and Joanne Zulauf studied. *Photo by Cloyd Steiger.*

Below: Boeing is the city of Renton's biggest employer. The Renton plant started out making bombers for World War II before converting to commercial planes in the 1950s. *Photo by Clifford B. Ellis.*

On Tuesday morning, December 16, 1969, Edward Stewart reported for his job at Chapman Electric. After checking in, he walked through a drizzle for a couple of blocks to the river. Stewart wanted to check the fishing conditions. He hoped to drop a line in after work.

He strolled down Williams Street to the muddy trail that led northwest along the west bank of the waterway. As he passed the Veterans of Foreign Wars building at 55 Williams Street, he saw something in the brush. Stewart peered closer; it looked like a mannequin, he thought. He examined it closer, and his heart rate quickened when he realized what he had found: it was a body, mostly nude and definitely dead.

Stewart backed away and rushed toward Chapman Electric. On the way, he came across his friend Richard Niemi.

"I think I found a dead woman back there," he told Niemi, still not believing what he was saying.

"Take me there," Niemi told him.

The two of them made their way back to where Stewart had seen the body. Niemi was also shocked.

They rushed to Chapman Electric and Stewart's boss, Mr. Dombrauski. They told him what they'd found.

"I'll call the police," Dombrauski said, reaching for the phone.

The call crackled over the Renton police radio frequency: "There's a man at Chapman Electric that advised that he found a female, believed to be deceased, half nude, near the river. Mr. Dombrauski was advised to have this man remain in the store until officers arrive."

Renton police officers Ray Smith and Dave Saude responded. They arrived at Chapman Electric and met Stewart, still shaken by his discovery. He led them to the body south of where a railroad trestle crossed the river.

Officer Smith touched the lifeless nude body and found it to be cold and stiff. He immediately asked for detectives to respond.

In 1969, the Renton Police Department was a small operation. There was no homicide unit. The few detectives on the department were generalists. Very few murders happened there. They often went five or six years with none. When there was a murder in Renton, it was usually a "smoking gun" type, where the suspect was evident from the beginning. This case had all the makings of a "whodunit." Cases like this are much more complex; the officers had no experience in these types of murders.

There were five or six detectives on the entire department, and all who were on duty responded to this scene.

Official Portrait of "Renton's Finest"

For the first time in a couple of years Police Chief C. S. Williams assembled members of his department for a formal photograph for The Record-Chronicle and the Sheriff and Police Reporter. The picture is by Ted Gatz and shows 59 members of the department, 50 officers and the nine women employes together with Mayor Donald W. Custer, Councilman Charles Delaurenti, chairman of the council's Police Committee, and Al Noble, chairman of the Police Civil Service Commission. Missing are Capt. W. E. Frazee and Patrolmen Claude Evans and Richard Nibarger.

From the left are:

Front row: Don Smith, James Foust, Robert Anthony, John Pavone, Robert Vaughn, William Brooks, Bradley Tofthagen, Wayne Fassett, Joseph O'Neil, Charles Swartfager, Frank Cooper.

Row 2: Sgt. George Gomez, Capt. K. M. Furseth, Capt. A. J. Brattus, Ass't. Chief F. A. Henry, Councilman Delaurenti, Chief C. S. Williams,

Mayor Custer, Chairman Noble, Capt. E. K. Henry, Lt. H.M. Edman, Sgt. W. J. Tracey, Sgt. Vincent Hansen.

Row 3: Parking Checker Warren Marshall, Sgt. Dale Orr, Sgt. James Bourasa, Sgt. John Buff, secretary Dora Blanchard, clerk-dispatchers Joan Merritt, Virginia McDaniels, Louise Craft, Sue Hawkins, Betty Mattison, Dorothy Dixon, Glenna Little, clerk-steno Winnifred Jones, Harold Caldwell, Sgt. T. A. Romano, Sgt. James Phelan.

Row 4: Donald Dashnea, Thomas Bingaman, Robert Fritsvold, James Goodwin, Emmett Kindle, Robert Margraf, Arnold Hubner, Robert Leyerle, Jon Northrop, William Bronsema, William File, parking checker Raleigh Stone.

Top row: Eric Bearscove, Earl McKenney, Sid Journey, Richard Mechan, Steve Bakko, Edward Combs, James Sundvall, Barton Dailey, W. L. Hume, Donald Persson, Joseph Henry, David Smith, Raymond Sande.

RENTON HISTORICAL SOCIETY

The Renton Police Department in 1968. Just over fifty sworn officers made up the ranks. *Courtesy of* Renton Record Chronicle/*Renton Historical Society.*

Detectives Don Dashnea and Wally Hume were among the first to arrive. Hume was new for a detective. He had only five years on Renton PD and had made detective after two years. "Everybody just seemed to want to tell me what they'd done," he later said, explaining his success as a detective.

Dashnea and Hume stood back and looked over the scene. They were joined shortly by the other detectives and Captain Bill Frazee, who took command of the crime scene.

The trail leading to the body was muddy; scrub brush and scotch broom lined the sides. The victim lay to the southwest of the path that paralleled the Cedar River. They could see what looked like drag marks leading from the trail to where the body lay, a little over thirty feet away.

The marks were uniform; it looked as though the killer had dragged the victim to her current location after she was unconscious. It didn't appear that she had struggled while being dragged; in fact, there was no sign the victim had struggled with her attacker at all.

The body was a white female, nude from the waist down other than a pair of white stockings. Her legs lay spread apart. She wore a gold pullover

The scene where Carol Erickson was found murdered along the Cedar River in Renton, Washington. *State of Washington v. Gary Gene Grant.*

sweater, pulled up, exposing her bra. A pair of blue jeans and women's panties were lying a couple of feet away. Without touching her, they could see marks around her neck. Her shoelaces lay nearby; it appeared they might have been used to strangle her. Also nearby was a brown leather ankle-high women's shoe, the shoelace removed. The other shoe was near the start of the drag marks; it was also missing a lace. A navy-blue coat lay several feet away, near the east slope of the railroad tracks west of the body.

After measuring and photographing the jacket where it lay, officers picked it up and went through the pockets. In the left pocket, they found a small photo book. Inside the photo book, they found a Washington driver's license with the name Carol Adele Erickson on it. The photo looked like it could be of the dead woman, but they couldn't be sure.

Detective Arnold Hubner arrived. After looking at the area around the body, he fanned out, looking for other evidence. He walked a worn

Looking north from the Erickson murder scene at the path Carol took from the library. *State of Washington v. Gary Gene Grant.*

path between the river and Logan Avenue to Williams Street. Partially concealed under some brush, he found a manila envelope. Inside were notebook papers, including a handwritten recipe for Irish potato soup, as well as other international recipes. The name Carol Erickson was scribbled at the top of each page.

Also inside was a letter apparently written by Erickson to Dan Kingen. The message closed with, "Well, I'd better get home now. I'm at the library. I walked over here by the river just to watch a pair of ducks swim down."

Officers spotted narrow tire tracks in the mud near the river that looked like they were from a small car. They photographed the tracks and then cast them in plaster.

Investigators for the King County Medical Examiner's Office arrived and did a scene examination of the body. There was a stab wound in the middle of the victim's back, as well as the furrow, presumably from shoelaces that had been around her neck. After placing her in a body bag, they took her

Right: Police found drag marks in the mud, indicating Carol Erickson's body had been moved after she was attacked. *State of Washington v. Gary Gene Grant.*

Below: Renton police at Carol Erickson's murder scene. *State of Washington v. Gary Gene Grant.*

Drag marks can be seen from Carol Erickson's body. *State of Washington v. Gary Gene Grant.*

to the King County Medical Examiner's Office, then located at the top of Queen Anne Hill in Seattle.

Dr. Gale Wilson had been with the King County Medical Examiner's Office (previously the Coroner's Office) since the early '30s. He had conducted thousands of autopsies during his long tenure, which would continue into the late '70s. Though he went about his business in an orderly

Left: Carol Erickson was just nineteen years old when she was murdered on December 15, 1969. *Courtesy of* Renton Record Chronicle/*Renton Historical Society.*

Below: Detectives found fresh tire tracks near Carol Erickson's body. They never matched them to a car. *State of Washington v. Gary Gene Grant.*

and unemotional manner, he had many times been witness to the evil that people do to each other.

He made a cursory examination of the body when it arrived. It was frigid, he noted, and the body had fixed rigor mortis, an indication that the victim had been dead for several hours. Her hands extended above her head. Livor mortis (purple discoloration of the body) told Dr. Wilson that she'd lain on her back for an extended time after death.

He looked at her clothing. He saw that the back of the sweater was bloodstained from a stab wound there, just to the right side of the midline of her back. He saw two distinct ligature marks around her neck; she'd been strangled with something other than hands. He guessed the time of death as sometime before 9:00 p.m. the night before. He scheduled the autopsy for the next morning.

Back at the scene, Detective Arnold Hubner used a metal detector to scour the scene for other evidence, especially the murder weapon. He didn't find anything.

Medical examiner investigators remove the body of Carol Erickson from her murder scene. *Courtesy of* Renton Record Chronicle/*Renton Historical Society.*

Detectives used metal detectors to search for the knife used to kill Carol Erickson. *Courtesy of* Renton Record Chronicle/*Renton Historical Society.*

Other detectives took up the task of determining if the dead girl was indeed Carol Erickson. Detectives Don Dashnea and Earl McKenney went to the address listed on the driver's license they'd found in the photo book. They knocked on the door but got no response.

A neighbor was home across the street. They walked over and spoke to the resident, Frank Miles.

"We're looking for Carol Erickson," Dashnea said. "Do you know where we might find her?"

"Carol lived there with her parents," he told them. "She graduated from high school last year. She lives somewhere else in Renton, but I don't know where. Her father's name is Art. He works at the First Baptist Church on Langston Road. He's the custodian there."

Dashnea and McKenney drove to the church. There is nothing worse that can happen to a parent than to lose a child, and when they spoke to Arthur Erickson and told him Carol may have been murdered, he was devastated.

Erickson then made the most difficult call of his life. He had to tell his wife that their precious daughter was dead. She immediately drove to the church. Dashnea asked them to go with him to the morgue to identify the body.

Today, forensic science has advanced so much that in-person identification of dead bodies is rarely done. In 1969, the only way to conclusively identify a body was fingerprinting, and Carol had never had hers taken. It's a terrible thing to see a loved one dead, but to see them in a morgue, the violence committed against them visible, is inconceivable. Reverend Camper from the church accompanied them for this horrible task.

When her parents saw Carol's dead body on the stretcher, they broke down. If the detectives had any inkling that Carol's parents had anything to do with Carol's death, it disappeared upon seeing the devastation on their faces.

"Last night," Mrs. Erickson told them through tears, "I was writing Christmas cards at about 6:45. I had a strong premonition that something was wrong, but I didn't know what it was. After about a half hour, the feeling went away."

"Carol lives in an apartment on Airport Way," Arthur Erickson told the detectives. "She goes to Renton Vocational College. She's taking culinary arts classes. She graduated from high school last year and started going to school there. She moved out of the house just after graduating."

They told the detectives that Carol worked at Kingen's Restaurant in downtown Renton, right next to her apartment on Airport Way.

Arthur gave the detectives a photograph of their daughter.

They could think of no one who would have done this. "Everyone liked Carol," Arthur said.

When Dashnea and McKenney saw the photo Arthur Erickson had given them, they were taken aback. They recognized Carol. They often had lunch at the school in the food preparation area and had seen Carol there before. She was vivacious, with a smile for everyone.

The detectives returned to the scene and told Captain William Frazee what they'd learned.

"Go up to the vocational college," he instructed, "and see what you can find out."

Dashnea went to the college, this time accompanied by Detective Harold Caldwell. The staff at the school directed them to a couple of people who knew Erickson.

The first was Robert Jaslawski. He told them he was friends with Erickson, though not romantically involved. He had a different girlfriend, Julie Bosely. Bosely lived in an apartment on Airport Way in Renton—the same building in which Carol lived. Jaslawski attended food preparation classes with Carol. He and his girlfriend were in a small circle of friends who Carol hung out with.

"Carol has a boyfriend," Jaslawski told the detectives, piquing their interest. Murders like these are almost always committed by someone close to the victim, such as a boyfriend. "His name is John Wilcox, and he lives in the same building, near Julie.

"John and Carol argued yesterday," he added. "They left school at about eleven o'clock in the morning. John was supposed to take Carol to work at Kingen's Restaurant, next to their apartment building, and they were arguing when they left. They do that all the time. Carol was interested in marriage; John wasn't."

"Carol used to go with a guy named Jim Williams," Jaslawski added. "She was supposed to see him last Friday night. He just got out of the service. They hadn't seen each other for a year."

He told them Carol lived with a girl named Bonnie Holms, who went to school somewhere in Seattle and worked at the employment office.

"Carol told me Monday morning she was going to go to the library that evening to work on a project for school."

The library was a short distance from Carol's apartment. It had been built a couple of years earlier spanning the Cedar River. The path along the river where her body had been discovered led right to it.

Detectives Dashnea and Caldwell drove to the Maplewood Golf Course, where John Wilcox, Carol's boyfriend, worked as a chef in the clubhouse.

The entrance to Renton Public Library. People outside on the day Carol left reported suspicious individuals standing near the entrance. *Photo by Cloyd Steiger.*

The Renton Public Library was built across the Cedar River a couple of years before Carol Erickson was murdered. *Photo by Cloyd Steiger.*

"We're investigating a murder," they said. "We think the victim is Carol Erickson."

Wilcox's face blanched, and he appeared physically shaken. He slumped into a chair. For a couple of minutes, he couldn't speak.

"Do you mind coming with us to the police station so we can talk about this?"

He told his supervisor he was leaving and went with them.

"When did you last see Carol?" Dashnea asked Wilcox in the interview room at the police station.

"Yesterday at about eleven-twenty in the morning," he said. "I gave her a ride from the Renton Vocational College to Kingen's Restaurant. We'd been arguing that morning on the way there. She wanted to go steady, but I didn't want to. She was crying when she got out of my car."

"How long have you known Carol?"

"We met last September at Renton Vocational. We were both taking food preparation courses. We started dating in January. We've been going semi-steady since then. She was always on me to go steady, but I didn't really want to. We got in arguments about that, but it was never physical. We'd just yell at each other."

John Wilcox, Carol Erickson's boyfriend, worked in the clubhouse at Maplewood Golf Course. Gary Grant also worked there briefly. It was across the Cedar River from where Grant killed Scott Andrews and Bradley Lyons. *Photo by Cloyd Steiger.*

"She was very possessive," he continued. "She'd be perturbed when I wanted to go out with my buddies for the evening. She demanded a lot of attention and got irritated when she thought I wasn't giving her enough."

"Did you know her to drink?"

"She didn't drink much," he answered. "Maybe a little wine from time to time, but only a little bit. She told me she didn't like to drink because it made her ears burn.

"She was a little high-strung. She couldn't sit still for more than twenty minutes or so. She'd go for a walk or a drive when she was restless."

"How was she around strangers?" they asked.

"She was overly trusting," he said. "She didn't seem to think about her own safety. She had no problem walking in dark and eerie places. I warned her about that, but she just laughed it off.

"She didn't like that I drank. She wanted to be active in church and wanted me to be too. We never argued about religion, but that's one of the reasons I didn't really want to go steady."

"Do you know who she went out with before you?"

"She went with Jim Williams. He's in the service, but I don't know which branch. Jim Tate is in the air force. He was in North Africa, but he was home on leave recently. I think he went back on the first of this month, and Dan Davidson. He's the nephew of Bob and Martha Kingen, who own the restaurant. He's in the navy, but he's home on leave."

Wilcox told the detectives about letters Carol had received the previous summer from a secret admirer.

"The letters were anonymous. They weren't lewd or anything, but the guy wanted to go on a date with Carol. He also went to Renton Vocational and told her to wear a blue flower in her hair if she wants to go out.

"I thought I knew who sent the letters, and I confronted him and told him to knock it off. She didn't receive any letters after that."

"Tell us what you did yesterday," the detectives said.

"I left my apartment at about six-fifty in the morning. I drove some people to their jobs. Carol was in the car in the front seat, and after I dropped the others off, we went to school.

"Like I said, I drove her to Kingen's, and we got there at eleven-twenty, then I drove back to the school. I got there about eleven-thirty.

"I left the school about one in the afternoon. I went to the Highland's post office and then went to the bank to cash a check. I then went to a car wash up there and washed my car. I got home about one-forty-five or two.

Carol Erickson shared this home with her longtime friend at the time she was murdered. *State of Washington v. Gary Gene Grant.*

"At about two-ten, I left for my job at the golf course and punched in. I punched out at about nine-thirty. I went home.

"When I got to my apartment, I saw that the lights were on in Carol and Bonnie's apartment, but Bonnie's boyfriend's car was in the lot, so I didn't stop by.

"When I got to my apartment, I talked for a minute to Julie Bosley, who lives next door. Then I went over to Kingen's at about ten. I met Jeff Zubrod and Craig Pagel and had a drink with them. I went back to my apartment at about eleven.

"At six-fifty-five the next morning, Bonnie told me that Carol hadn't returned home last night and was still not there.

"I know she liked to take long walks," he told the detectives, "and she sometimes walks to the library by taking the trail that runs along the river."

"Are you willing to take a polygraph if we ask you to?"

"Yes," he replied.

Detective Hubner spoke with Bonnie Holms, Carol's eighteen-year-old roommate. Bonnie was distraught after hearing the news of Carol's death. She had been sedated by a doctor.

"I've known Carol for fifteen years," she told Detective Hubner. "We met through our church."

Bonnie told Hubner what she knew about Carol's relationship with John Wilcox. "They had several arguments over the last three months," she said.

She told Hubner the last time she saw Carol was December 15 at about 6:45 a.m. when she left for school.

"When I got home yesterday at about six in the evening, I found the note Carol left saying she was going to the library."

She told Hubner about Jim Williams. "He was an old boyfriend of Carol's. He came home from the military. He tried to contact Carol a couple of nights before. He was upset that she had a boyfriend."

She also told Detective Hubner about Jim Mount. He'd come to the apartment the night before, along with another friend, looking for Carol. Bonnie told them Carol had gone to the library. They left to go there. They came back a little later, saying they hadn't seen her there. They stuck around until about 9:15 p.m. in case Carol returned but finally gave up and left.

Shortly after they left, Jim Williams and a friend named Don Collier also came to the apartment looking for Carol. They left at about ten o'clock.

The detectives were interviewing everyone with any connection at all to Carol. That evening, they spoke to Walter Warrick.

Warrick was going out with Bonnie Holms, Carol's roommate.

"I was at the apartment every night this last week," Warrick told them. "Last night I got here about five-thirty. When I came in, I found a note on the table for Bonnie from Carol. It said she'd gone to the library."

"Were you here all night?" the detectives asked.

"I went to Safeway to buy some biscuits, but I was only gone a few minutes." Warrick retrieved the grocery receipt for the biscuits and gave it to the detectives.

"Do you have any idea who would do something like this?" they asked him.

"I have no idea," he replied.

The detectives asked if he'd be willing to take a polygraph test about this.

"Absolutely," he said.

In the meantime, Hume and McKenney went to Kingen's to interview the staff there. Several people said they saw Carol when she left work the day before; no one had any idea who would do something like this.

On the morning of December 17, 1969, Dr. Gale Wilson conducted the autopsy on the body of Carol Erickson. Detectives Dashnea, McKenney and Jim Foust and Officer Joe Henry attended.

Renton Girl, 19, Murder Victim

Renton police are investigating the slaying of a 19-year-old Renton girl who lived in the 400 block of Airport Way — the second female murder victim from that block in the past five months.

The body of the girl, identified as Carol A. Erickson, was discovered about 8 a.m. yesterday, partly hidden in the weedy overgrowth of a railroad track embankment just south of the Cedar River and east of Logan Avenue South.

Miss Erickson, identified by po-

lice as a kitchen helper at Kingen's Restaurant, 423 Airport Way, had recently moved into a cabin behind the restaurant. She was the daughter of Mr. and Mrs. Arthur C. Erickson, 13434 SE 180th St.

In the previous slaying, the body of Mrs. Marjorie Thomson — shot once in the back — was found in the trunk of her car in Olympia Sept. 5. Mrs. Thomson disappeared Aug. 23.

Prime Suspect in Case

The Thomson slaying remains under investigation. Police say there is a prime suspect in the case. The cause and time of death in

the Erickson murder had not been officially determined yesterday. But Renton detectives said she may have been strangled and / or stabbed.

An autopsy is scheduled this morning, county medical examiner's deputies said.

Police were interviewing the man who found the body yesterday, but declined to identify him at the time.

Apparent Assault Victim

Miss Erickson appeared to be the victim of an assault, according to Renton police.

The body was partly disrobed when discovered, police said.

Detectives speculated that Miss

Erickson may have been walking along a footpath beside the Cedar River when the attack came.

Grooves in the path, partially filled in by rain, appeared to angle from the path to the underbrush where the body was found — about 20 yards south of the path. Police speculated she may have been dragged from the path.

Nearly a dozen patrolmen and detectives combed the area in a grim search during yesterday's steady drizzle.

An electrical metal detector was brought from the City Water De-

partment to aid in the search for evidence.

Officials at Renton Vocational-Technical School, which she had attended the past two years, said she had been in classes all day Monday. She was enrolled in commercial cooking courses there.

Spokesmen at the school described her as "very sweet-natured."

Miss Erickson attended Kent schools and was a 1968 graduate o Kent-Meridian High School. Offi cials there described her as a goo student and said she had been activ in orchestra and Girls' Club.

Council Delays Decision

Above: The murder of Carol Erickson shocked the residents of the sleepy town of Renton, Washington. *Courtesy of* Renton Record Chronicle/ *Renton Historical Society.*

Right: Dr. Gale Wilson had been the coroner/medical examiner in King County since the early 1930s. He performed the autopsies on all four victims in this case. *Courtesy of the* Seattle Times.

After the clothing was removed and the body was photographed and X-rayed, Dr. Wilson made his observations. In addition to his previously noted observations of her injuries, he found evidence of a sexual assault.

There was no underlying damage under the ligature marks on her neck. The airway was intact but narrow.

He examined the stab wound to her back. Its angle was downward at about forty degrees. It severed the seventh rib and pushed a large fragment of the bone into the pleural cavity around the lungs. It also nicked the sixth and eighth ribs. The wound penetrated the lower lobe of her right lung, into the inferior vena cava and the right atrium of her heart. The depth of the injury was fifteen millimeters (about six inches). There were seventy-five milliliters of blood in the sac of her heart and eight hundred grams in the pleural cavity. The stab wound had been fatal.

Dr. Wilson collected various samples for later testing.

The detectives made a plea to the public. They cooperated with the *Seattle Times*, the evening newspaper in Seattle. In an article published on December 19, Renton police shared with the media that they believed Carol had been to the Renton Public Library. They pleaded with readers who may have been at the library that Monday night when she was killed to contact them.

A few people came forward. A couple of them believed they had seen Carol that night. They may have, and a few reported nefarious people they saw in and around the library that night, but they had little or no information about who may have killed her.

There was a buzz around the Renton police station. It was a small police department, and everyone knew everyone else. The murder was a hot topic of conversation at the department. Everyone wondered who had killed Carol Erickson.

Dozens of tips poured in over the weeks following Carol's murder. Detectives followed up on all of them. They were all dead ends.

After a while, the tips coming in tapered to a trickle. Renton detectives were no closer to solving the murder than they were on the morning they stood over Carol's cold body.

JOANNE

September 19, 1970, was a chilly, breezy, end-of-summer day in Renton. The high temperature that day rose only to sixty degrees, with wind gusts of about fifteen miles per hour.

Seventeen-year-old Joanne Marie Zulauf lived in a quiet neighborhood in unincorporated King County, just outside the city limits of Renton, with her brother, John Zulauf; mother, Virginia; and stepfather, Ralph Thompson. A small girl standing only five feet, two inches and weighing just over 110 pounds, Joanne wore her reddish-brown hair in a short bob. She was a vibrant young woman.

Joanne planned to meet a friend for a bike ride after dinner on that Saturday late afternoon. She left the house, telling her parents she was going to go for a walk before they sat down to eat. She walked out of the house and turned left.

When more than an hour passed and Joanne didn't come home, the Thompsons became concerned. It wasn't like her not to return when she said she would.

Ralph jumped into his truck and drove around the neighborhood looking for her. When he came back home, having found no trace of her, Virginia jumped in with him to keep looking.

They drove onto a dirt road leading into a wooded area north of their house in the direction Joanne had walked when she left home. As they did, they passed a man they didn't recognize walking out of the woods. They looked at him closely.

Right: Joanne Zulauf told her parents she was going for a walk before dinner in 1970. She never returned. *State of Washington v. Gary Gene Grant.*

Below: Joanne Zulauf lived in this home with her mother and stepfather when she disappeared on a Saturday afternoon. *Photo by Cloyd Steiger.*

By ten thirty that night, Joanne had still not come home. Fighting off panic, her parents called the King County Sheriff's Office. The operator took the information but didn't dispatch a car. Teenage kids go out on their own all the time; she'd probably be back. The operator told them to call back if she didn't show up.

By the next morning, there was still no sign of Joanne. The Thompsons were frantic. She'd never done anything like this. They called the sheriff's office again.

At 3:30 p.m., Sheriff's Deputy L.M. Moffet arrived at the Thompsons' home. After talking to them about Joanne and her disappearance, he spoke

Joanne Zulauf was last seen walking down this sidewalk on a Saturday afternoon in 1970. She would never be seen alive again. *Photo by Cloyd Steiger.*

to Joanne's friend Robin Williams, with whom she had planned to go on a bike ride the day before.

"We just made those plans a short time before she went for a walk," Williams told the deputy.

Moffet didn't like it; this wasn't your typical teenage girl runaway. There were no apparent problems with her parents, no fights or disagreements. Also, she'd made plans to go on a bike ride with her friend shortly before she went missing. A person planning on running away wouldn't do that. She hadn't dressed in warm clothing, even though it was relatively cold out, and had left her purse with her driver's license, car keys and glasses behind.

Moffet called for others to help him try to find Joanne.

Donald Hodges lived a block north of the Thompsons. The day before, he'd told them he saw Joanne walk past his house while he was in the front yard. Moffet went to speak with him.

"I was in my front yard when I saw the girl walk by," he said. "I recognized her. I've seen her walk by before. I know she lives down the street. I didn't think anything of it. She went up a trail into the woods by my house under the power lines."

About fifteen to thirty minutes later, Hodges saw Ralph Thompson drive down the road past his house and park by an old tree-trimming pile that was near the dead end at the end of his street.

"About a half hour later," Hodges continued, "I went for a walk. It's something I do almost every night. I went down the same trail I saw the girl go on. I didn't see her."

When Moffet got back to the Thompsons' house, he got a call from Sergeant George Helland.

"I've called for search and rescue," Holland told him. "They're on their way with dogs."

Civilian volunteers make up search-and-rescue teams. Many of them have tracking dogs. They are organized and drill frequently and are available for searches like this one. At 6:30 p.m., the first of the dog teams arrived. Moffet showed them the wooded area near the house that he wanted to be searched. They began searching, along with other team members who trickled in.

Just after midnight, almost thirty-six hours after Joanne left home, Moffet received a call from one of the searchers.

"You need to come down the trail into the wooded area," she told him. "We found something."

Moffet walked down the trail, where he came across the search team.

"She's down here," a searcher told Moffet before leading him into the gully in the woods. About three hundred feet from the gravel road that bisects the forest was the nude body of Joanne Zulauf; her bra and panties lay about six feet from her body.

"Everyone stand back," Moffet told the dog teams, "and move as little as possible."

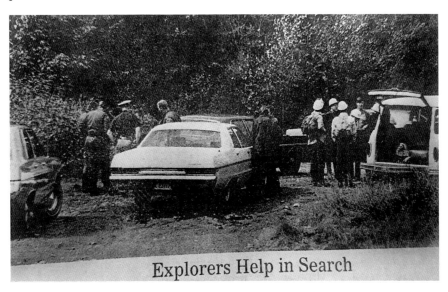

Detectives called in Explorer Scouts to look for evidence at the Zulauf murder scene. *Courtesy of* Renton Record Chronicle/Renton Historical Society.

Joanne Zulauf's bra was found a few feet from her murdered body. *State of Washington v. Gary Gene Grant.*

He made a full circle around the body, shining his light in front of him to avoid stepping on potential evidence. He approached from the downhill side, the route least likely to have been taken by the killer. He peered at her face. He'd seen a photo of Joanne earlier at the Thompsons' house. He was sure this was her. He reached down to check for a pulse but found her body cold and hard. He backed away and walked back to his patrol car, leaving two members of the search team to guard the scene.

Once he got to his car, he found Ralph Thompson and Jean Johnson, Joanne's stepsister, standing nearby.

"I'm sorry, Jean," Moffet told her. "We've found Joanne, and it's not good. I'm afraid she's dead."

He called for detectives to respond.

While Moffet waited in his car, he could hear a despondent Ralph Thompson saying to Jean, "I told them so. I told them to search this area first. I told them so. This is the exact spot where Mr. Hodges said he saw Joanne enter the woods."

When the detectives arrived, Moffet filled them in on what he knew.

Because it was dark in the woods, the detectives decided not to try to process the scene that night. It would be too easy to miss what could be a crucial piece of evidence in the dark. They posted a deputy to guard the scene and waited until first light to start working.

Once the sun came up, they went to work, first photographing the area and the body. They found two footprints in the mud, which they photographed and later lifted with a plaster cast.

Joanne's body was nude, and the detectives couldn't see, on initial observation, any wounds. There was blood in her nostrils and mouth, but that was likely purge, something that often happens after death but is not a sign of injury or assault. It looked as though the killer had dragged Joanne's body from the trail area to where it lay now.

Joanne had been wearing a watch and earrings when she left the house. Later that morning, medical examiner personnel moved Joanne's body; those items were missing. The investigators searched the area more thoroughly. They didn't find the missing jewelry or any other evidence.

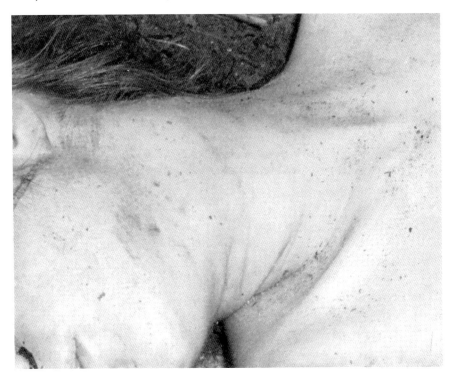

Ligature marks can be seen on Joanne Zulauf's throat. *State of Washington v. Gary Gene Grant.*

They called Explorer Scouts—troops of teenagers who volunteer to assist with outdoor scenes, especially to locate evidence—to the scene to help with a grid search of the area. The scouts did a shoulder-to-shoulder search, covering virtually every square inch of the area. They didn't find any evidence.

Detective Sensebach left the scene to go to the Medical Examiner's Office to watch the autopsy of Joanne's body. The autopsy was started at 2:30 p.m. on September 22, 1970. Again, the pathologist was Dr. Gale Wilson, the same doctor who conducted the autopsy on Carol Erickson. Dr. Wilson found that Joanne's body was in full rigor mortis but that it was beginning to fade. Rigor mortis generally disappears after about twenty-four hours, depending on the conditions. This meant she'd likely been dead for more than a day.

There were petechial hemorrhages on her face from the chin to the hairline. The conjunctive area of her eyes showed marked petechial hemorrhages as well. Petechial hemorrhage is a sign of strangulation, caused by cutting off the blood vessels near the surface of the neck, which sends blood back to the heart and lungs for reoxygenation. The arteries, more rooted in the structure of the neck, still carry freshly oxygenated blood to the brain, but with the cutoff of the veins, there is nowhere for it to go. The pressure builds in the small blood vessels, and they begin to rupture, causing small red splotches.

Her lips were blue, but there was no evidence of injury. There was a bloody ooze that trickled from her nose and corners of her mouth down both cheeks, but mainly to the right; this was likely purge, mentioned earlier.

The tip of her tongue was bitten between her tightly clenched teeth.

Dr. Wilson found a superficial wound to her head, consistent with being struck by a hard object. Dr. Wilson also found injuries to her neck that led him to believe she had been strangled, possibly with a belt. He also found evidence she had been sexually assaulted.

He ruled the cause of death to be strangulation during an attempted rape. The manner of death was homicide.

Meanwhile, the detectives canvassed the neighborhood. One neighbor told them he'd seen two boys on bikes in the area of the homicide on September 20. He recognized one of the boys as Dennis Kreider. Dennis was a freshman at Hazen High School, which is about a mile from the crime scene. Detective D.L. Harrison went to the school on the morning of September 22 to talk to the boy. Harrison found Kreider very cooperative.

"I was riding my bike with my friend, Bill Nause, at about five-thirty in the afternoon," Kreider said. "We drove down 104th to the end of the street.

There's a wood chip pile there. We rode up onto the pile and were looking out over Hidden Valley, directly below us. We saw two boys, about eleven to thirteen years old, on the other side of the valley. They yelled to us, 'Hey boy! There's a motorcycle down in the valley!'

"It was too far away to tell who they were. We didn't see or hear a motorbike.

"We'd seen a hawk earlier, and we were looking for it when we heard yelling coming from down in the valley to the right of where we were.

"I heard a girl's voice yelling. The only thing I could make out was her saying, 'Get back!' The rest of the words were muffled. The girl's voice sounded between fourteen and fifteen years old.

"I heard a deeper voice at the same time, but I couldn't make out what he was saying. It sounded like the voices were traveling a long distance, and they were arguing back and forth. We didn't think anything of it, and Bill and I left the area and went home."

Sergeant Jim O'Brien spoke to Ralph Thompson to find out more about the day Joanne went missing.

"On Saturday, my wife and I went to Tiger Mountain looking for pigeons," he said. "The weather was bad, so we came home at about twelve-thirty to one o'clock. Joanne was here when I got home. She was just finishing up doing schoolwork when we got back.

"Joanne had plans to go bike riding with Robbie Williams. When she was done with her work, she sat around and got impatient. She left to go for a walk. She said she'd be back in ten minutes. She left and didn't come back. We thought she may have gone to Robbie's. My wife called there several times.

"We went looking for Joanne about six-forty-five. We took the dog in our pickup truck and drove down to the end of 104th. There's a dirt road that runs north and south. We turned north on the dirt road and saw someone about two hundred feet away. As we got closer, we saw it was a man. He seemed to have just popped out of the woods."

"Could you describe him?" O'Brien asked.

"He was between thirty-five and thirty-eight years old, five foot seven to five eight. He had darkish-brown hair. He was starting to get a high forehead. He had on faded blue jeans, which were very clean. He had work clothes on, and they were very neat. He had on dark oxfords; they may have been black. He wasn't wearing a hat. When we got close to him, he turned his head toward the woods. I would recognize him if I saw him again."

"Are you sure the man you saw wasn't Mr. Hodges?" O'Brien asked.

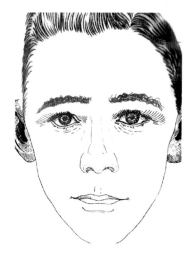

Police developed a composite sketch of a suspicious person seen by Joanne Zulauf's parents walking out of the woods where her body was later found. *State of Washington v. Gary Gene Grant.*

"No, we saw Mr. Hodges later walking on 126th.

"My wife called the police at about ten o'clock that night, and they took a report. The next day, I went walking back in the woods looking for her, and then the officer came and they started their search."

Sergeant O'Brien also interviewed Robin Williams.

"I got home from Bellingham at about two o'clock," she told him. "I called Joanne at three-thirty. We talked for about fifteen minutes. We were talking about a friend's wedding and that her parents were planning on going on a one-year trip with their trailer and that she would live in the house and pay fifty dollars a month.

"We made plans to go bike riding when I finished my homework. Joanne was in a good mood.

"I called back about ten to five. Mrs. Thompson told me Joanne went for a walk and would be back soon. She said she'd have Joanne call me.

"At about twenty to seven, Mrs. Thompson called and said Joanne hadn't come back from her walk; she wanted to know if she was at my house. She said she wasn't worried because Joanne may have met some friends and gone for a ride.

"Mrs. Thompson called back at about eight-twenty. She said she was worried because Joanne hadn't come home and she hadn't heard from her.

"I called some friends and asked if they'd seen or heard from Joanne; no one had.

"I called Mrs. Thompson again at seven the next morning. She told me she hadn't heard anything.

"I went to school at Renton Vocational School. Later that day, Mrs. Thompson showed up there looking for me, Connie Smith and Debbie Hague. She was worried about Joanne and had no idea where she was. That was at about ten-forty-five in the morning.

"At four o'clock, we went to Joanne's house and waited. The dogs came and started searching. We went to Lake Boren to look there.

"Mr. and Mrs. Thompson were worried. They were sure she hadn't run away. She liked both her parents."

The detectives had heard about possible drug use by Joanne. They asked Robin about that.

"Last December, I went to a basketball game at Hazen High School. A friend of mine had a hit of acid with her. I took a fourth with some coke. It didn't have any effect on me.

"Later that month, or in early January, Joanne and I went with a couple boys to Snoqualmie Pass. We had a hit of mescaline. Joanne and I each took a hit. It had an effect on us. This was Joanne's first experience with mescaline, but she'd been smoking grass for about a year. We also used mescaline and acid a couple times after that. We got it from a guy who was at our friend's house."

The detectives were intrigued by Williams's recollection of Joanne's drug use. Could this have a bearing on her murder? The vast majority of murders involve drugs on some level. They had little else to go on at that point.

Rumors were circling that a nineteen-year-old man was telling his friends that he had found Joanne's body before the police did. They jumped on the lead right away.

"I just said that," he told the detectives, "so I'd look like a big man to my friends. It isn't true."

"Where were you on Sunday?" they asked.

"I was home playing football in my yard with my cousins," he said.

They checked it out. It was true.

On September 28, detectives sent twenty-five items to the FBI crime lab in Washington, D.C., in a letter to J. Edgar Hoover. At that time, there were very few items of evidence that could be conclusively linked to a murderer; none of the evidence they sent carried that possibility. Hoover, a notorious micromanager, personally responded to every correspondence between the FBI and local detectives about the evidence in the case.

Detective D.L. Harrison got a call from a teacher at Demitt Junior High School named Tom Companion.

"I live on the edge of the woods where that girl's body was found," Companion said. "On that Sunday, I was home watching the replay of the Husky football game."

Companion told Harrison that between five and six o'clock on the evening Joanne went missing, he saw a man walk out of the woods near his house. He thought the man was at least thirty-five years old, perhaps a bit older. He was of average height and weight with dark hair that looked thick and curly on the sides. He wore a dark-colored hat—the kind golfers wear in bad weather. He wore a jacket that had sleeves that looked lighter than the body of the coat.

"He came out of the woods east of where the body was found," Companion said. "He walked by my driveway and then went east on 100th. He went right by two young boys riding Stingray-type bikes.

"I'd never seen this guy before, and not since. I saw the sketch in the newspaper, and he didn't look like that, but I thought I should tell you about it."

Companion told the detectives that he was colorblind, so he wasn't sure about any colors.

Harrison went to see Donald Hodges. They asked to see the clothing he wore on his walk. He showed them a "semi-dress" straw hat, a gray-green nylon jacket, dark pants and shoes.

"Did you walk over by the Companions' house?" he asked Hodges.

"Yes, I went over by there and down 100th. I saw Mrs. Companion in the living room window when I went by."

"Did you see any kids on bikes?"

"No, I didn't," he replied.

They later spoke to Companion's wife.

"I just had a baby, so I was home recovering," she said. "I was on the couch near the front window. When the Husky replay came on, it was about five-forty. I got up and went to the bedroom to lie down. I didn't see anyone walking outside the house."

Detectives D.L. Harrison and Vince Pellegrini canvassed the neighborhood where Mr. Companion said he saw the man walking. Though they spoke to several neighbors, none remembered seeing anyone walking in the area or anything else suspicious on that day.

Detectives called Diane Williams. Williams had attended a high school football game the Friday before this incident with Joanne.

"She seemed happy," Williams told them. "After the game, we bought a pack of cigarettes. She took a few of them. That was the last time I saw her."

The detectives knew of the murder of Carol Erickson in Renton several months before. There were similarities they couldn't ignore: both victims attended Renton Vocational College. Both were walking in wooded areas when they were apparently attacked. The scenes weren't too far apart. Both victims had been dragged from their assault sites to where their bodies were found. They called Renton police detectives to compare notes. They spoke to Don Dashnea about the cases, but there was nothing conclusive. They just filed it away in the back of their minds.

Victims Carol Erickson and Joanne Zulauf both attended the Renton Vocational School (now Renton Technical College). There's no indication they knew each other. *Photo by Cloyd Steiger.*

Much like the Erickson homicide, King County sheriff's detectives received many early leads that seemed promising at first. One of those leads involved Calvin Durham. Durham was a known criminal with a long rap sheet. Detectives heard that he was in the neighborhood on the day Joanne went missing.

They looked for a booking photo for him. The only one they found was from 1957.

Durham's ex-wife lived in the area. She told the detectives he had showed up at her house in early September.

Detective Harrison met with Mrs. Thompson. He showed her the 1957 photo of Durham. She told him the picture was not of the man she and her husband saw walking in the woods. Because of the age of the photo, the detectives weren't sure.

Harrison interviewed Betty Frodsham, Durham's ex-wife. She told him that she married Durham in 1952 and that they were only married a year. She became pregnant and had a son, Rick. Durham saw Rick just one time, when the boy was five years old. Rick was eighteen years old when Durham visited in September

She told Harrison that Durham had a bad-conduct discharge from the U.S. Air Force in 1950. He was arrested several times after that for minor offenses in Kelso, Longview and Spokane. He broke out of jail in Kelso, and when he was arrested, he was sent to the McNeil Island Penitentiary. After his release, he went to California and went back to prison, though she didn't know why.

When he showed up, he wanted to take his son with him for a few days. He said he was going to Port Angeles. Frodsham agreed.

Durham returned to Renton in mid-September. He wanted to get money out of Rick's savings account. Durham told her Rick had gotten a traffic ticket and also needed money for school.

A week later, Frodsham got a call from Ulla Stamper in Port Angeles. She said that Durham had been staying with her there. Stamper told her that while he was there, Durham raped her daughter. Frodsham told the detective Durham had a brother in Forks who owned a welding shop. She thought he might be staying there.

A few days later, Rick called Frodsham. He told her he and Durham had driven to Tulsa, Oklahoma. He wanted to let her know he was fine. She told him about Joanne Zulauf's murder. Rick said he knew Joanne slightly.

A couple weeks later, Durham called Betty Frodsham. "He was angry and threatened me," she told the detectives. "Rick came on the phone. He sounded scared." Rick said he couldn't tell her where he was, but he was okay.

"Have they solved Joanne Zulauf's murder yet?" he asked.

The Durham lead was intriguing. He was known to be violent, had been in the area at the time of the murder and had an indirect connection with Joanne, however tenuous. At that point in the investigation, few leads seemed promising. This was the exception. So much so that Detectives Harrison and Pellegrini made the two-hour drive to Port Angeles, on the Olympic Peninsula. They met with Ulla Stamper.

"I met Cal Durham in downtown Port Angeles," she said. "We became good friends, and I gave him money for his business. I gave him about $3,000 and a 1964 two-door Pontiac.

"After knowing him for about two months, I realized he had a mental problem. He would just fly off the handle and yell, using foul language.

"Cal told me he and another man robbed a bank. He said they got about $30,000. He didn't tell me where it happened or if he got caught.

"One day we were at Crescent Lake. Cal pulled a gun and put it to my head. He told me if I told anyone about him, he'd blow my head off. I was able to grab the gun and throw it in the lake."

"Do you know where his business was?" the detectives asked.

"He said it was in Forks, but I don't know the address."

Long before becoming famous as the setting for the book and movie series *Twilight*, Forks was a sleepy logging and fishing town. Then it was just a small burg on the tip of the Olympic Peninsula, the farthest point northwest in the continental United States.

"He drank a lot. He had a drink when he woke up in the morning," Stamper said.

She described the time around the murder.

"He picked up his son in Renton and was at my house. On September 17, Cal and Rick went back to Renton to pick up clothes for Rick. They showed up back here on Monday, September 21, at about three-thirty in the afternoon. Cal told me that they got to Forks on Sunday night and were too tired to drive any farther, so they stayed at his brother's house. When I saw him, he had a scratch across his forehead and across his nose."

That didn't make sense. The detectives knew that to drive from Renton to Forks, he would have had to drive through Port Angeles first. Why would he tell Stamper they'd made it to Forks and were too tired to drive to Port Angeles?

"A couple days later," she continued, "Rick told me he walked in on Cal and my daughter making love. It turned out, he raped my daughter. There's a warrant out for his arrest because of it now."

Mr. Frodsham called Detective Harrison.

"I want to call my son," he said. "I'll ask him about when he and Cal were here. If he's lying, I'll be able to tell."

He called back a couple days later.

"I spoke to Rick and talked to him about this investigation. He said on September 18, he and Cal were in Forks with Cal's brother. They stayed there overnight. Ulla Stamper came over that Friday night, and Saturday they all went back to Port Angeles. They stayed there through Sunday, September 20.

"Rick is flying home in a few days," Frodsham said. "I'll bring him in for an interview when he gets here."

When Rick arrived, Harrison took him and Mr. Frodsham to Seattle police headquarters. Seattle police detective Dewey Gillespie conducted a polygraph examination on Rick. After the test, Gillespie told Harrison he didn't believe Rick had any knowledge of the homicide.

Though a decision like that based on a polygraph alone is always a mistake, the detectives believed they'd reached another dead end in a case full of dead ends.

As with the Erickson case, the leads slowly ebbed until they trickled in only occasionally and, finally, nearly stopped altogether. Despite a tremendous amount of work and doggedly following up on every likely lead, the detectives were no closer to solving the murder than they were the night they were called to the scene.

THE BOYS

On Tuesday, April 20, 1971, six-year-old Bradley Lyons jumped out of bed. Though he'd typically have to go to school on a day such as this, today was a teachers' conference day; there was no school.

Brad dressed in a gold, gray and white long-sleeved polo shirt, with olive green perma-press pants. He went to the kitchen of his home in Renton and sat down for breakfast: bacon and eggs with toast and milk.

At about ten o'clock in the morning, he donned an olive-green reversible coat with the quilted side out and then rode with his mother and his sister Kelly to a hardware store on East Valley Highway to buy some lumber for his dad. They returned home and unloaded the wood before driving to the service station where his dad worked to swap out his dad's pickup for the family car. They then returned home.

"I'm going out to play," he told his mother.

It was about eleven o'clock in the morning.

"He didn't say who he was going to play with," his mother later told detectives, "but I assumed it was Scott Andrews. He always played with Scott."

She watched out the front window of their home in a quiet suburban neighborhood as he walked in the direction of Scott's house. She saw Brad and Scott outside a few minutes later. A little while later, she looked out the window. She saw Brad and Scott walking from the house, northwesterly toward a wooded area.

She would see neither of them alive again.

SCOTT ANDREWS, ALSO SIX years old, lived near Bradley Lyons with his parents, Sharlene and Keith Andrews, and two brothers, Aaron, age four, and Jay, three.

On that morning, Scott asked for Alpha-Bits cereal without milk for breakfast. He often ate cereal plain like that.

Scott dressed himself that morning in a white T-shirt under a light orange shirt that had the outline of a car stitched in the left side near the top. He wore jockey shorts and bronze-colored denim pants that had a hole in the right knee and no belt. He wore rubber-insulated Pac boots with flat laces.

Scott and Aaron went outside to play at about ten-thirty that morning. Scott put on his avocado-colored nylon coat with a hood. They played in a vacant lot behind their house with five or six other neighborhood kids. After a bit, Scott came in for cookies. He grabbed enough to share with his friends before going out again.

"I didn't tell him to stay in the yard," Sharlene Andrews later told detectives. That would haunt her for the rest of her life.

At about eleven-thirty, she looked out. She saw Aaron playing in the yard with his friend Jeff. Scott was nowhere to be seen.

At eleven forty-five, Sharlene needed to leave to get her driver's license renewed. She looked for Scott but still didn't see him.

She called Chloe Andrews, Brad's mother.

"Is Scott over there?" she asked.

"I saw them playing outside about a half hour ago," Chloe told her.

Sharlene waited for her husband to get home. She wasn't concerned. Renton still had a small-town feel; nothing bad ever happened there.

Sharlene's husband, Keith, came home.

"I don't know where Scott is," she told him.

Keith went out looking for him.

By five o'clock that afternoon, they were scared. The boys weren't usually gone that long. They called the King County Sheriff's Office to report that their son and Bradley Lyons were missing.

The close-knit neighborhood commenced a search of the area. Though the boys sometimes played for long periods, they never stayed out after dark.

Eventually, the King County Sheriff's Office coordinated a more organized search. They called in search-and-rescue personnel. Forty members of the Spring Glen Fire Department helped too. Searchers worked around the clock, checking the area ponds, swollen with recent rains, but a sleepless night for the Lyons and Andrews families passed with no sign of the boys.

Bradley Lyons and Scott Andrews were best friends. On a day with no school in 1971, they were brutally murdered. *Courtesy of* Renton Record Chronicle/*Renton Historical Society.*

Wednesday night passed with the families trying to cope with their dread, but still, no sign of the boys came.

"When they went missing," Renton detective sergeant Jim Phelan later said, "we all thought they'd probably fallen in the river." The woods near the quiet neighborhood where the boys lived was formidable, with old-growth Douglas fir and a thick canopy.

On Thursday evening, Firefighter Daniel Auburn, assisting in the search, was walking under the power lines near the Royal Hills Apartments. He walked down the hill and then into a swampy area, crossed it and then walked up to a hill on the other side. He circled back to the power lines when he came to a level spot. He looked to his left, spotting a pair of boots. He then saw the head of a small blond boy. He walked within six feet of the boy but didn't go any closer.

The boys' bodies were found in these woods, adjacent to the Royal Hills Apartments. *Photo by Cloyd Steiger.*

The dread the families felt that evening came true; he'd found the body of a small boy wearing a white-striped T-shirt. Auburn called his supervisor. Soon, the body of the other boy was found nearby, partially covered with plants and dirt. There were no signs of life.

The searchers secured the area and called for police.

King County sheriff's deputy Richard Nicholson arrived, followed shortly after by Sergeant George Helland. They realized that where the boys were found was in the city of Renton. They called Renton police.

Renton detectives Don Dashnea, Arnold Hubner, Wally Hume, Harold Caldwell, Joe Henry and John Pavone arrived at about 9:25 p.m., followed shortly by Sergeant Jim Phelan. Caldwell and Pavone were assigned to a narcotics enforcement squad supervised by Phelan and wouldn't typically respond to a scene like this, but this was the worst murder in the history of the city, so everyone got involved. They set up a command post about two hundred yards north of the Royal Hills Apartments.

"If you wanted to give Renton an enema," Detective Pavone said later, describing the Royal Hill Apartments, "that's where you'd stick the hose."

The route from the command post to the scene was another two hundred yards away, down a low grade. When Don Dashnea got to where the bodies lay, he saw them on the side of the hill. They were mostly nude with just their heads showing from under dirt, ferns and brush. The killer had covered the bodies, which is sometimes an indication that the killer wanted to psychologically "undo" the murders.

Scott Andrews's and Bradley Lyons's bodies were found in the woods two hundred yards from the Royal Hills Apartments. *Photo by Cloyd Steiger.*

After the devastating find of the murdered boys, police formulate a plan. *Courtesy of* Renton Record Chronicle/*Renton Historical Society.*

Bradley Lyons still wore the striped long-sleeved polo shirt, pulled up to his armpits, that his mother described him wearing when she last saw him. There was dried blood around his face, from the bridge of his nose to his right ear. Some sort of cord was around his neck. Detectives later discovered it was from a Venetian blind.

Scott was face-down, his underwear twisted around his ankles. His T-shirt was wrapped around his throat, as though he'd been strangled with it. He had what appeared to be stab wounds to his chest and neck.

"When you get two little boys like that," Sergeant Phelan said, "it's pretty horrible."

The detectives began photographing and diagraming the scene. They found a shoe print in the mud near the bodies. It looked like a heel with a circular pattern to it—perhaps a suction cup. They made a plaster cast of the print.

At 2:20 a.m., investigators John Lombardini and Norm Willis from the King County Medical Examiner's Office arrived at the scene. After the boys' bodies were photographed and examined, they were transported to the medical examiner's office.

The detectives secured the crime scene at 3:30 a.m.

Dr. Gale Wilson began the autopsy on Bradley Lyons at 6:00 a.m. on the morning of April 23. Bradley was forty-seven inches tall and weighed fifty pounds. The body was in complete rigor mortis. Dr. Wilson noted that the body had apparently lain on its back since the time of death, which, based on the circumstances and condition of the body, he estimated at about 5:00 p.m. on April 20.

Bradley's shirt was up to his chin, but his arms were still in the sleeves.

Dr. Wilson observed some dried bloody mucus on the face and in his left ear. He had petechial hemorrhaging across the middle of his face, inside the eyelids and in the conjunctivae of his eyes. He had bruises on his upper and lower lips, and his tongue protruded from between his clenched teeth. Two small clutches of blowfly eggs were under the left side of his chin.

Dr. Wilson cut the Venetian blind cord from around Bradley's neck. It was wound around four times. He taped the cut ends to prevent unraveling and turned the cord over to Renton detectives who were present at the autopsy. He found petechial hemorrhages in the larynx and epiglottis, as well as under the vocal cords, indicating asphyxia. He ruled that Bradley died of strangulation. The manner of death was homicide.

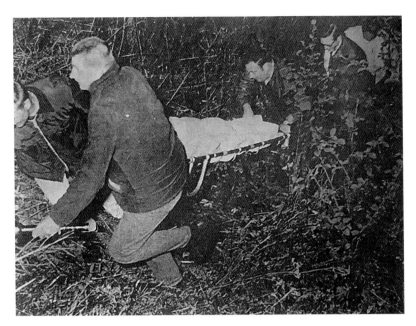

The murdered bodies of Scott Andrews and Bradley Lyons are removed from the scene. *Courtesy of* Renton Record Chronicle/*Renton Historical Society.*

When Sergeant Jim Phelan saw the bottom of Gary Grant's tennis shoes, he immediately recognized the print from the crime scene of the boys' murder. *State of Washington v. Gary Gene Grant.*

The most hardened detectives were devastated to find Bradley Lyons's and Scott Andrews's murdered bodies. *Courtesy of* Renton Record Chronicle/*Renton Historical Society.*

At 7:45 a.m., Dr. Wilson began the autopsy of Scott Andrews. Scott was also forty-seven inches tall. He weighed forty-nine pounds. Postmortem lividity showed that he had been lying face-down.

Jockey shorts were down over his ankles, and a bloody white T-shirt was twisted about his neck and tied in a knot behind his left ear. He had bruising to his left cheek and both lips. Like Bradley, his tongue was protruding through his teeth, slightly to the right of midline.

He had three stab wounds to his chest. The first was a relatively superficial wound into the fatty tissue around his left clavicle. That wound was not fatal. The second wound was thirty centimeters long, penetrated in a downward fashion. It nicked the left lung, penetrated the heart and stuck into the vertebrae. This wound was fatal. The third wound was similar to the second, just over the left nipple, through the left lung. This wound was also fatal.

Dr. Wilson's findings were that Scott died from stab wounds to both lungs and his heart. The manner of death was also homicide.

Back near the scene, detectives had the difficult job of interviewing both boys' parents.

"Bradley was a very active boy," Chloe Lyons told them between sobs. "If I had to discipline him, he would fight me before I could spank him. I feel very certain that if anyone were trying to harm Bradley, no matter how big they were, he would try to fight back very hard.

"Bradley would never go off with a stranger," she assured the detectives. "He wouldn't even go with relatives he hadn't seen in a while."

Sharlene Andrews, Scott's mother, also spoke with detectives. "Scott was very much a person of habit," she told them. "He was neither exceptionally smart or dull. He was very shy around strangers; even around some neighbors."

The Renton detectives searched the area around the scene several times over the next few days looking for more evidence—notably the knife—with several using metal detectors. They had no luck.

On April 28, Captain Frazee asked Explorer Search and Rescue personnel to comb the scene near where the boys' bodies had been found. Explorers are volunteers, usually mid- to late teenagers, led by adults. They are similar to Boy Scouts, but their primary mission is looking for lost persons and sometimes evidence at a crime scene. They grid off an area and search shoulder to shoulder. They can cover large areas and don't often miss much.

The tactic paid off.

Around two o'clock in the afternoon that day, Emmett Husa, an eighteen-year-old member of the group, found a hunting knife in the brush, not far from the crime scene. The knife had a five-and-a-half-inch blade with a ten-and-a-half-inch overall length. There was black "friction tape" wrapped around the handle. Husa called for his team leader, Larch Douglass, who went to the spot where the knife had been found. When he saw the weapon, he radioed for Renton police to respond. Detectives Don Dashnea and Harold Caldwell and evidence officer Joe Henry arrived to photograph and collect the knife.

Concerned parents meet with police to discuss safety for their children after Lyons and Andrews were found murdered. *Courtesy of* Renton Record Chronicle/*Renton Historical Society.*

The citizens of Renton were shocked at the murders of Scott and Bradley. It was the first double murder in the city's history; that the killing was of two young boys made it even worse. Parents clamored for information that would help keep their children safe from whoever did this.

On that same Tuesday afternoon of April 20, 1971, Judy Reed was in her office on West Valley Highway in Kent, just south of Renton. She was speaking to Bart Giard, a customer of the business. The front door opened, and a man walked in. He looked dazed.

"Can I have a drink of water?" the man asked.

"There's a drinking fountain in the hall," she said, pointing the way. The man walked out to where she'd indicated.

"I'm not leaving until that guy is gone," Giard told her when the man went to the hall.

After a moment, the man returned.

"Where am I?" he asked.

"You're in Kent," Reed answered.

"Am I still in Kent?" he asked.

"Where do you want to go?"

"Snoqualmie," he replied.

She and Giard gave him directions to Interstate 405 north to head to Snoqualmie. He didn't acknowledge them and walked around her office before returning to her desk.

"It's such a long story," he told her. "I don't want to go into it now. I don't feel well. Is there a hospital near here?"

"Valley General is the closest hospital," she said. "Go to the corner by the telephone company and take a right…"

"I'm not asking for a ride," he interrupted. "Just tell me where it is, and I'll get there."

He walked out of the office. They last saw him walking north on West Valley Highway.

"What an odd man," she remarked.

CALLY ZIGALLA WAS NINETEEN. She worked at the admitting desk in the emergency room at Valley General Hospital. She was there on April 20 at about 5:20 p.m. She noticed a man seated in a chair in the waiting area. She walked up to him.

"Can I help you?" she asked.

"I'm waiting to see a doctor," he said.

"Why don't you step over to my desk," she said. "I'll take your information.

He did as she said and sat down in a chair at the desk.

"What do you want to see a doctor about?" she asked.

"Every once in a while, I get to the point where I have to go to the hospital," he said. "They admit me to the psychiatric ward for a couple weeks, and then I feel better."

"What's your name?" she asked.

He hesitated and then took out his wallet and went through it but didn't give his name. After a moment, she got up.

"Just wait here," she said.

She went to get the triage nurse, Elizabeth Sullivan.

"There's a guy here who wants to see a doctor," she told Sullivan, "but he won't give me his name."

"I'll go speak with him," Sullivan told her.

She found him seated at the admitting desk. She took a seat next to him.

"How can we help you?"

He sat for a long time, not responding.

"I'm no good," he said finally. "I'm a con man."

He rambled on about this and that, not elaborating on what he meant. Finally, after about ten minutes, he handed Sullivan an identification card with the name John Chance.

She took him back to a treatment room and took his blood pressure. When she did, she noticed scratches on his arms and that his clothing was wet.

"Why are you wet?" she asked.

"I've been out in the rain," he said.

She believed he was emotionally ill.

She left him and went to get a doctor. She found Dr. Donald Rohrssen. "We have a patient," she told him, "that seems to be emotionally disturbed."

She described her interactions with Chance and said that he refused to identify himself when he first presented in the emergency room. She told Rohrssen which room Chance was in.

"What brought you into the emergency room today?" he asked Chance.

"I'm all mixed up, and I need help," Chance told him.

Chance was "violently agitated, but coherent; quite rampant in his discussion."

He told Dr. Rohrssen that he'd considered killing himself, but he had no guts.

"How long have you been mixed up?"

"For a long time."

"Have you seen any physicians about this?" Rohrssen asked.

"I've seen several physicians," Chance told him.

"Which physicians have you seen?"

"I'd rather not say," Chance said, "but I've been seen at the Tacoma Crisis Clinic."

"What's bothering you the most that brought you here today?"

"I've considered hurting children."

Doctor Rohrssen went over Chance's background with him and then asked, "Why do you think you're no good?"

"I've been given several chances," he said. "But every time things are running smooth, I deliberately do something to ruin it."

"Why did you come in today?" Rohrssen repeated.

"I'm afraid I'll hurt children," he answered. "I want publicity. I have a feeling that I'm identifying with the Manson family; like Manson is controlling my mind.

"I've seriously considered killing myself, but I don't have the guts to do it."

"Are you seeing visions or hearing voices?" Rohrssen asked.

"No."

Rohrssen noticed the scratches on Chance's arms. They looked consistent with being in blackberry bushes or something like that. They seemed relatively fresh—certainly less than twelve hours old.

"How did these happen?"

"I was walking through the brush," Chance told him.

"How did you get here to the hospital?" Rohrssen asked him.

John Chance walked into the emergency room of Valley General Hospital the night the boys went missing saying he wanted to hurt children. The investigation took a turn. *Photo by Cloyd Steiger.*

Chance was not responsive. Dr. Rohrssen thought he seemed evasive about the time just before his arrival there.

"Like I told you," he said, "I'm no good. I let people down. I do things wrong."

Rohrssen asked again what made him come to the hospital.

"I feel like I want to hurt children," he said again.

Dr. Rohrssen went back to the nurses' station. "Give him an injection of Thorazine and then move him to the security room."

Rohrssen thought that Chance was either suicidal or homicidal. He wanted to take every precaution.

Rohrssen made arrangements for Dr. Martin Hershberg, a staff psychiatrist, to take over as Chance's attending physician. After Chance was transferred to Dr. Hershberg for care, Rohrssen went about seeing other patients. He thought little more about Chance until he was home the following Thursday.

That morning, his wife took their daughter to school. When she got home, she mentioned that the two little local boys who were missing still hadn't been found. It was at that moment that John Chance's statement to him about wanting to hurt children came to his mind. He'd come to the hospital on Tuesday night—the same day the boys went missing—and in his opinion, Chance was homicidal. Since a large search contingent had been looking for the boys and still had not found them, Rohrssen was pessimistic that harm hadn't come to them.

But there was a problem: Dr. Rohrssen wasn't sure if he was bound by doctor/patient privilege. He wasn't sure he could tell the police what he knew.

He called the hospital and spoke to nurses there. He asked them to contact attorneys representing the hospital and get their opinion about him sharing the information he knew. Later that day, he heard back from the attorneys. They told him this could fall under the battered child law; they would call the police for him.

Detective John Kelly from the King County Sheriff's Office called Rohrssen and arranged to meet him at the hospital that evening.

At the time of the call, Kelly was at the scene where the boys' murdered bodies had been found. He told Renton detectives about the person at the hospital. About 9:30 p.m., Kelly and Renton detective Wally Hume left the scene to go to Valley General, where they interviewed Drs. Rohrssen and Hershberg. After speaking with them, all four went to Chance's room in the hospital.

Chance had been given a slight sedative at the hospital before the interview.

Wally Hume advised Chance of his constitutional rights. Chance told the detective he understood his rights.

They noticed scratches on Chance's arms, legs and forehead.

"On Monday, I was in Seattle," Chance told the detectives. "I wanted to commit suicide. I went to my mother's house up on Denny Street, but I didn't go in, I just kept walking. I walked out toward Sicks Stadium toward Renton on Rainier Avenue. I slept in the swamps and fields. At one point, I saw a river."

"Were you ever in a wooded area?" they asked.

"I don't think so. I saw a boy, and he gave me a Philips-head screwdriver."

"Did you tell the doctor when you got to the hospital that you wanted to hurt children?"

"I may have said that," he answered, "but I don't think I hurt anyone."

He said he talked to a boy in a brick house.

"Were you ever near power lines?"

"I don't know," he said.

"Do you know an area called Royal Hills?"

"No."

"We found the bodies of two little boys," Detective Kelly told him.

"I have a mental block," Chance said. "I can't say whether I hurt those boys or not, but I can't imagine that I did."

At that point, Chance became visibly upset.

"I wouldn't have any reason to hurt any children," he said as he reached for a drink of water. "I've been in many mental institutions. I do relate myself to Charles Manson and the Tate murders. At one point in my life, I thought I was from Saturn. Other people control me and my mind. I forget things from time to time. One time I showed up at work in my pajamas."

After the interview, Dr. Hershberg agreed to have Chance transported to Harborview Medical Center in Seattle, which had a more advanced psychiatric care area.

Detective Hume collected the clothing Chance was wearing when he came to the hospital as evidence.

They called for a patrol officer to come to the hospital and guard Chance and follow him to Harborview when he was transferred. Renton police officer Claude Evans took that call. He waited at Valley General Hospital until an ambulance arrived to take Chance to Harborview just before 11:00 p.m.

Once at Harborview, a doctor interviewed Chance. Afterward, he told Officer Evans that there was insufficient cause to admit him. Officer Evans asked to speak to the psychiatric resident. The psychiatrist, Dr. Petrich, also interviewed Chance. He refused to admit Chance, citing security issues with the psychiatric ward, from which patients had escaped before.

After contacting his superiors, Dr. Petrich admitted Chance.

Detectives Hume and Kelly returned to the crime scene and stayed there until it was secured at three o'clock in the morning.

At about noon, they heard that Harborview was going to discharge Chance. They went to the hospital and picked him up and then drove him to the Renton Police Department. Detectives Dashnea and Hume interviewed Chance again at the Renton police station.

During the interview, Chance intentionally lied several times. He told the detectives, when they began questioning him, that he would do so. "Although the investigating officers believed the individual to be psychotic," Hume noted in his report, "he is also quite intelligent."

At about 1:15 p.m., Sergeant James Phelan and Detective Wally Hume took Chance, along with Irene Taylor, a friend of Chance's, to the area of the Royal Hills Apartments and the crime scene

During their conversation, Chance told Phelan that he had murdered the two boys, saying that he strangled one with a cord and stabbed the other with a hunting knife. He described the knife as being about eight inches long with a five- to six-inch black handle.

At the scene, they tried to get Chance to show them the route he had taken to the boys and where he went before he arrived at Valley General Hospital. Chance wasn't sure he'd be able to retrace his steps but told the detectives he would try.

"He was one you could have led him into believing anything," Sergeant Phelan later said about Chance. Phelan didn't like it. "You felt funny about it," he said.

"I met the boys near some cut wood," Chance told Phelan and Hume. "I remember a red wagon being nearby."

He led Phelan back into the woods, taking the trail near where the boys' bodies were found. When he got to a spot close to that point, he stopped and then looked around, trying to remember the route he took. He walked to the right for a short distance and then angled to the left, uphill through the brush.

Phelan and Chance waited at the top of the hill for Hume and Taylor to catch up; it was harder for her to walk through the brush.

Chance talked about the incident.

"After killing the boys, I placed them side by side," he said. "Their clothes were off, so I covered them."

"Did you completely cover them?" Phelan asked.

"No," Chance answered, "everything but the heads."

"What did you cover them with?"

"Humus and ferns," Chance replied.

"Did you use anything else?"

"Leaves and boughs."

"What did you do then?" Phelan asked him.

"All I wanted to do was get far away," Chance answered.

"Were you afraid?"

"No," he said.

When Hume and Taylor arrived at their location, Phelan asked Chance to try to find where he put the knife. Chance led them back downhill, through brush and seemingly oblivious to obstacles. He checked several tree stumps and finally ended up on a trail about two hundred feet from the scene. He seemed bewildered. "I don't think I'll be able to find it," he said.

"Didn't you follow a trail?" Phelan asked him.

"I made my own trail," he replied.

They left the area and went back to the Renton police station.

Chance was later booked into the Renton City Jail for investigation of murder for the killing of Bradley Lyons and Scott Andrews.

The Renton detectives tried to find out what they could about Chance, his background and personality and where he'd been in the days before Bradley and Scott disappeared.

Detectives Dick Nibarger and Pavone interviewed Joseph Tomac.

"On Monday the nineteenth between six and seven in the evening, I was washing down the front steps to my house [in Renton]," he told them. "This guy came up to me and said, 'I know this sounds silly, but can I have a drink of water from the hose?'

"I gave him the drink. He said thanks and left."

Tomac gave the detectives a description of the man, though he couldn't remember if he had a beard.

"He was acting peculiar," Tomac added. "Like he was drunk or something, but I didn't smell alcohol on him."

He told the detectives the man walked down the hill after leaving his yard. He hadn't seen this guy before or since and wasn't sure he would recognize him if he saw him again.

Daniel Milliken was a friend of Chance's. He was interviewed by Detective McKenney.

"I've known John Chance for about ten years," he told them. "We met at the American Lake Veterans Hospital. We were both being treated for a nervous disorder. Since then, we've been good friends and see each other when we can."

"When was the last time you saw Chance?" McKenney asked.

"I last saw him on Saturday night, April 17," Milliken said. "He visited me and my friend at our apartment on Capitol Hill in Seattle."

"Tell me about that day."

"As I recall, John came to the apartment at ten-thirty at night. He was acting strange, in that he was very quiet and not his normally jovial self. I tried to talk to him about it but finally decided to leave him alone, and he slept on the couch. I went up to my room and watched TV until about one in the morning.

"When my friend and I got up in the morning, John was gone. He had planned on playing in a chess tournament that day, but he left his suitcase with all his chess equipment in it. He'd originally planned to stay through the twentieth for the tournament."

On April 27, Chance went through a psychiatric evaluation by Dr. Jack Klein. In his report to the prosecutor's office, Dr. Klein described the interview as "extremely disorganized because of Mr. Chance's mental condition. At times he rambled, he was quite verbose, and seemed confused about the timing of things that any other single factor."

Chance told Dr. Klein that he'd been born in Atlanta and was raised in Colorado, California and Washington, where his family moved when he was twelve.

"My mother is alive and well," he told Dr. Klein. "She lives in Seattle, but I haven't seen her for several months."

He told the doctor that he had never known his father. "I had a stepfather from 1942 to 1955. I got along well with him." His stepfather died in 1955.

Chance said that he'd completed high school. Afterward, he went to Portland University for two years and then transferred to Columbia University in New York City, where he received a bachelor's degree, maintaining a 3.1 grade point average.

Chance told Dr. Klein that he'd been treated at several mental facilities over the past few years, including several in Washington and one in California. He was always told that he suffered from schizophrenia.

He received electric shock treatments at Western State Hospital in Washington and Patton State Hospital in California and as many as thirty shock treatments at the American Lake Veterans Hospital. He was confused about the dates but guessed he'd spent about five years in the various hospitals combined.

He married a girl he met when he attended Columbia University. That marriage lasted only a year. He reported that he had a son out of wedlock.

He taught at the Issaquah (Washington) School for one year. He was terminated, he said, for giving a high grade to a "negro girl" for a paper that was considered pornographic. He then taught for six months at a school in Wapato, Washington, but he became "ill and was hospitalized."

After Chance was discharged from American Lake hospital, he got a job at a bakery but was fired for coming to work in his pajamas, though he told Dr. Klein he had no memory of this. He then worked a short time for Weyerhaeuser Lumber Company but lost that job because he "just began not to work."

He was in the Army Reserves during the Korean War and was activated for a year but never left the United States. He was discharged from the army with a medical discharge and awarded a partial pension for that.

Dr. Klein reported that "Mr. Chance's memory seems intact for both recent and remote events although he has difficulty with dates of events and the sequence of them happening. At the time that I talked to him, he was oriented as to the time, place, and person."

During the interview, Chance was extremely restless, frequently getting up and pacing the room. His primary concern was that he was constipated because he didn't get enough exercise in jail.

Dr. Klein asked him about the murders of the two boys. "He was aware of the fact two boys had been killed in the Renton area and that he was a suspect," Dr. Klein wrote in his report, "but he did not believe it was possible for him to have done such a thing."

Chance acknowledged that if he had done such a thing, the consequences would be long-term incarceration or death. Despite that, Dr. Klein reported, "he did not show the expected intensity of concern." Klein described his response as "a rather flattened, intellectual repetition of things he knew. He was much more concerned with exercise and his bowels, and whether I approved or disapproved of him personally."

Dr. Klein mentioned a series of strange mental phenomena, delusions and hallucinations that came up during the interview. Chance related a time when he was "looking into astrology" and someone mentioned to him that he was the son of Saturn. Since that time, he believed that maybe he was born on one of the rings of the planet and that being a Saturn person instead of an Earth person accounted for his inability to adjust to life on Earth.

He told Dr. Klein that he met Jesus Christ. He said Jesus is a man in Tillicum, Washington, who is six feet tall, has a beard and leads a group called Jesus' People. Chance tried to join, but they "laid hands on him," and he did not respond. They told him he was "too full of the devil" and rejected him.

He also believed he was then–Washington governor Dan Evans. He thought this because when he walked down the street, people stared at him. "At the time, I thought the people following me were bodyguards," he said.

"One time," he added, "I sat in my room for three days. I had a wonderful feeling, and I seemed to get the thought from God that he was the ruler of the world and controlling it with my mind. When nothing I thought about happened for a few days, I thought that may have been an error."

He told Dr. Klein that he sent and received messages with his mind. He said he received more than he sent. "I think you sent me a message that you hated me," he said to Klein. "Is that true?"

Dr. Klein assured him it was not.

"I think I'm half man, half woman," he said, "because they're keeping me on the women's side of the jail."

He thought the people in the jail were brainwashing him but then added, "Maybe I'm paranoid."

Chance rambled on with other nonsensical stories for some time.

At one point, he said, "I'm a sadist and a masochist."

Dr. Klein asked him about the time before he showed up at Valley General Hospital.

"I was in a chess tournament in Seattle on April 16, 17 and 18," he said. "As I walked out the door, I had a vision of God telling me I had won. At the tournament, I became angry at some of the referees, so I shouted at them and threatened them.

"After I left, I next recall being down on the waterfront near Ivar's [restaurant]. I jumped in the bay. Once I was in the water, I chickened out and climbed the ladder out.

"At the top of the ladder, a man asked if I was all right. He gave me a cigarette, and I walked away.

"I don't remember what happened thereafter," he continued, "except I wandered on and on, walked through woods and fields and brush.

"I tried to rest under a bridge at one time, and flopped in a field on another occasion, and slept in an abandoned truck another time.

"I was looking for water. If you're without food, you can live on only water for a period of time."

The next thing he recalled was going to Valley General Hospital.

"I think the doctor was Martin Bormann. I've always wanted to be a Jew."

He said he thought the doctor was Martin Bormann because he gave him a shot.

Dr. Klein diagnosed Chance with paranoid schizophrenia and opined that he'd had that condition for several years. Because of this, Dr. Klein believed that Chance "is not able to adequately participate in his own defense, nor is he capable, emotionally, of realizing his peril to an adequate degree.

"Since he is extremely prone to obey, as he says, the voice of God, the inspiration he receives directly from God and other mental telepathic messages and because of the period of extreme mental confusion starting in early April, being terminated by the shot of Thorazine given to him at Valley General, it would be my opinion, if Mr. Chance did kill the boys, he was at the time unable to tell the difference from right and wrong."

The last sentence was significant because it is the very definition of legal insanity, which is different from medical insanity.

"At the same time," Klein offered, "I would also be of the opinion Mr. John Chance was capable of committing such a seemingly purposeless act."

He concluded by recommending that Chance be hospitalized in a mental hospital until there was a high probability that he had made a complete recovery and would not relapse.

"In fact," Dr. Klein added, "pending new medical discoveries, in all probability, Mr. Chance should be hospitalized permanently."

ON APRIL 29, 1971, John Chance was formally charged with two counts of first-degree murder for the deaths of Bradley Lyons and Scott Andrews.

That same day, he was examined by another psychiatrist, Dr. Richard Jarvis. Jarvis said Chance was "courteous and cooperative, is articulate and quite intelligent."

After giving Jarvis the same background information he gave Dr. Klein, Chance spoke about the week leading up to the murders.

John Chance
He pleads innocent

"I came up from Tacoma on a bus on April 16 to go to a chess tournament," he said. "I stayed at the Ethelton Hotel. I had a good night's sleep, but I knew something was wrong.

"They put me in a trance at the tournament. A jury of my peers put the kibosh on me. I'd been bragging around that I was a better player than I really was. I was imagining that the Mafia was coming through the door. I ran from the tournament after my last move and spent a weird night on the streets of Seattle," he added, referring to Sunday night, April 18.

"I wanted to go to University Hospital," he continued, "but I didn't know how to get there, and I didn't have any cash. I thought that Irene [his latest girlfriend] was in dire straits, and I went to Swedish Hospital and asked to be hooked to a machine to save Irene. They told me to get out. I'd pissed my pants several times

John Chance confessed to killing Bradley Lyons and Scott Andrews. After Gary Grant confessed to those and the murders of Carol Erickson and Joanne Zulauf, the charges against Chance were dismissed. *Courtesy of* Renton Record Chronicle/ *Renton Historical Society.*

that night, something I'd never done in my life before, and that probably had something to do with them telling me to get out.

"I walked the streets like an automaton, and early Monday morning, I went to police headquarters but didn't talk to anyone there. Then I went to the bay and threw myself into the bay, but I thought better of it and climbed out.

"I went to my mother's apartment up on East Denny Way. When I walked in, she looked different. I thought she'd been harmed."

He told Dr. Jarvis that he had been "getting messages" to leave town.

"I started out Rainier Avenue," he said. "I felt that I was a cop-out to the chess community and had let them down. I also let my mother down by not coming over for Easter."

He told Jarvis he didn't know how he got to Renton but remembered buying a bag of jellybeans. He said he spent Monday night walking on rural roads and lying from time to time in fields. He said he "received messages" from passing cars and trucks.

When the conversation came to Tuesday, April 20, he said, "Now it's getting to be a blank. Maybe I'd better shut up.

"I know I'm a suspect [in the murders], but if I did commit the crime, I don't know it."

"Someone else must have committed the crime," Jarvis said of Chance, "and he's a suspect because he was a suspicious character who was wandering around and doing odd things."

He told Dr. Jarvis that he was far away from the scene when the crime happened. "I was down by the Boeing facility in Kent when the crime happened," he said. "I think I was brainwashed by the police; a picture was put in my mind," though he didn't allege any mistreatment or discourtesy by the police.

"I have a power to repel people and to attract women, but right now, as is always the case when I'm ill, I'm so constipated I can't think straight."

Dr. Jarvis concluded his report by saying, "If Mr. Chance did, in fact, commit the killings, I think it's probable that, even in his disturbed state, he had sufficient capacity to have the cognitive awareness of the act and its wrongfulness."

Chance was arraigned for the murders on May 3, 1971, represented by local public defender Frank Sullivan. He entered a plea of not guilty to the charges.

THE FIRST DOMINO FALLS

After collecting the knife at the boys' murder scene, the detectives took it directly to the Seattle police crime lab. Kay Sweeney was a criminalist at the lab. He examined the knife and processed it for fingerprints but found only smudges on the handle. He found traces of blood on the blade; it was type A.

Sweeney unwound the electrical tape wrapped around the handle with the hope of finding fingerprints on the lower layers. When it was removed entirely, he discovered a name was etched into the handle under the tape. The name was Tom Evenson.

Detectives identified Evenson as a twenty-year-old man who lived in the neighborhood. He was away in the U.S. Marine Corps in basic training in California at the time of the murders. He was to graduate in the next few days and was going to be home on leave after that.

On April 30, Evenson came into the Renton police station for an interview with Detectives Brad Tofthagen and Don Dashnea.

"I left for the marines on February 16," he told Tofthagen. "I was there until yesterday when I flew home."

"Tell me about a hunting knife you had with your name on the handle," Tofthagen said.

"I bought that knife at Ernie's Payless in Kent, sometime in November of 1969," he said. "I think I paid about a dollar-fifty for it. I don't remember the brand name of the knife, but it had a black plastic handle and a wide blade, about five inches long. On the end of the handle, there was a metal knob that was checkered and would screw off."

"In August of 1970, I sold the knife to a guy named Jerry Triplett. Jerry broke the handle and wrapped it up with black electrician's tape. The last time I saw Jerry with the knife was about November of 1970.

"Before I sold the knife, I put my name on the end of the metal knob. I'm pretty sure I used a hammer and punch to do that."

"Do you know where Triplett is now?"

"He's in Oregon, but I know he doesn't have the knife anymore," Evenson said. "I was there when he sold the knife to Jim Monger. He lives in a trailer park off Lake Washington Boulevard. He goes to McKnight Middle School."

Tofthagen showed him a photograph of the knife recovered near the murder scene.

"Is this the knife you're talking about?"

Evenson looked at the photograph.

"That looks like it," he said. "The only thing different is it looks like a different type of tape on the handle."

Later that morning, Detective Wally Hume and Sergeant Jim Phelan went to McKnight Middle School to interview Monger, a sixth grader there.

"I got that knife from Jerry Triplett," Monger said.

He described the knife in detail.

"Is this the knife?" Phelan asked, showing him a photo of the knife in evidence.

"Yeah, that's it," he said.

"What happened to the knife?"

"I have a friend who lives in the trailer park too," he said. "I was riding in his pickup truck. We were in his dad's red GMC pickup. I had the knife with me and laid it on the seat. When he let me off, I forgot the knife. That's the last time I ever saw it."

"What the guy's name whose truck you were in?" they asked.

"Gary Grant," he replied. "I asked Gary about the knife a couple times after that. He said his dad cleaned out the truck and found the knife and put it in his room. He said he didn't dare go in his dad's room to get the knife."

Hume and Phelan went to Grant's address in the trailer park at 2100 Lake Washington Boulevard, Space 59.

"We knew Gary's dad was a security guard," Phelan said. "Since he supposedly found the knife, we wondered if he might be the guy. We figured the boys might have gotten in the car with somebody like that, so Wally and I went out to the trailer park to confront the father and find out what happened."

Gary Grant lived in this trailer park along the shores of Lake Washington with his parents. *Courtesy of the Renton Historical Society.*

"John Chance was a nut," Phelan said, explaining why he and Hume still explored other possibilities regarding the murders. "He was one you could get to have led to believe anything."

They met with Glen Grant and his wife, Penny, Gary's parents.

"Is Gary around?" they asked the Grants about their nineteen-year-old son.

"He went to get his hair cut at Folks Barber College," Penny said. "He drove my husband's pickup."

They interviewed Glen.

"Did you find a knife in your pickup truck?" they asked him.

"No," Glen said. "I don't know anything about a knife in the truck."

He explained to them that he worked as a "private policeman" at Highline Police Agency in the Fairwood neighborhood of Renton.

They were still speaking with Mr. Grant when Gary returned home in the truck at about 12:15 p.m.

Sergeant Phelan went to speak to Gary away from his father. Though Phelan didn't know much about Gary, he did know a little. "He wandered around," Phelan said. "He was all over town. He even walked past my house [a little ways out of town] a couple times."

"I asked him to step from the truck and have a seat in the back of our police car," Phelan said. "As he got into the car, his shoe flipped up, and I saw the pattern on the bottom. There had been a shoe print at the scene, and I remembered it. The bottom of his shoe looked just like that print.

"I went back in the house and talked to Wally. 'We have to get out of here,' I told him."

"We're here about the knife Jim Monger left in your truck," Phelan said to Gary after he and Hume had returned to the car. "Where's the knife now?"

"I left it in the woods up there," he said, gesturing to the wooded area about the trailer park. "I camp out there all the time with other guys."

Phelan asked him to describe the knife. He gave Phelan a detailed description of the knife that was in evidence for the murder.

"Do you mind going with us to the Renton police station so we can get a statement from you about where you last saw the knife?" Phelan asked.

"Sure," Grant said.

They arrived at the police station at 12:34 p.m.

"Can I see the bottom of your shoes again?" Phelan asked when they were in an interview room.

Grant lifted his feet to show them to Phelan.

"Can I have you take them off?" Phelan asked.

Grant did as he was told, and Phelan took them from the room. He found Officer Joe Henry, who was handling the evidence for the case. "Compare these to the castings from the scene," he told Henry.

Henry took out the cast that had been made from the shoeprints at the scene. It was a perfect match for Gary's shoes.

Back in the interview room, Wally Hume continued interviewing Grant. He advised him of his constitutional rights; he said he understood.

"Tell me what you did on Tuesday, April 20," Hume said. "That was the day there was no school because of a teacher in-service day."

"In the morning," Grant said, "I worked for a while at the driving range near my house. From there I walked to Renton to maybe buy a pair of shoes and get a fishing license."

"How much money did you have on you?" Hume asked.

"I had five dollars," he said. "I went to several stores and then down by the Cedar River by Renton High School Stadium. I saw something floating in the river, and I walked down. I fell in and got soaked.

"After I got out of the river, I walked to Frankie's Serve-U Market on Park Avenue North."

He said that once he was at the store, he called his mother and asked if his dad could come get him. She told him his dad was asleep and wouldn't be able to.

"What clothes were you wearing that day?" Hume asked.

"Those same shoes I was wearing today," he said, "and I think these same pants and shirt I'm wearing today."

Hume showed Grant a photograph of the knife they recovered near the scene. "Is this the knife you had?"

"Yeah, that's the same knife," Grant said.

Hume had Grant sign the back of the photograph telling him he was identifying the knife as the one he'd owned.

"I have problems with my mother," Grant told Hume. "She has a drinking problem. I went to live with my sister in Portland, and she sent me to a psychiatrist. I was put in group therapy."

"Have you ever blacked out or had a time when you couldn't remember what was going on?" Hume asked.

"There was one time in school when I was in shop class," he said. "I had a knife in my hand at the time. I looked around, and I could see the other people, but I couldn't hear anything.

"Another time, a guy got mad at me and started yelling at me. When I looked at him, I saw my mother yelling at me instead of the person who was actually doing it."

"Did you ever have any urges to hurt anyone or yourself?"

"I don't want to hurt anyone else."

Hume noted that he didn't answer the question about harming himself.

"Did you hear about the two missing boys who were found dead?" Hume asked.

"Yeah, I heard about it," Grant said.

"The knife I showed you the photograph of, that you said had been in your possession, was found near the boys' bodies."

Grant became somewhat emotional.

"I wouldn't hurt children," he said.

"Would you be willing to take a polygraph examination about the knife and your knowledge of the murder of the two boys?"

"Yes, I'll take a polygraph," Grant said.

Outside the interview room, Hume and Phelan discussed the circumstances.

Grant had been the last person known to have possession of the knife. The shoes he had on were similar to the shoe prints left at the scene. He might have knowledge of the murders.

At about 2:30 p.m., Hume and Phelan drove Grant to Seattle police headquarters. They went to the second floor, where the polygraph section was, along with the crime lab.

George Ishi was a criminalist with the Seattle Police Department.

"Dewey Gillespie," the Seattle police polygrapher, "is out of the office," he told them. "I'm not sure when he'll be back."

Ishi set about trying to contact Gillespie.

"I got a hold of him," Ishi told the Renton detectives. "He said he can be here at 5:30 p.m. to give the test."

Grant was showing signs of strain and was getting a little emotional, the detectives noticed.

"Why don't you take him out of here," Ishi said. "Get him something to eat and let him calm down before the test."

They put him back in the car and drove to a Jack-in-the-Box restaurant on Capitol Hill. They went to the dining room and ordered food. While they sat and ate, they made general conversation but intentionally didn't talk about the crime or their investigation.

They returned to Seattle police headquarters at about 5:15 p.m. At around 5:45, Detective Dewey Gillespie, the Seattle police polygraph operator, returned. Hume spoke to Gillespie in his office while Phelan waited outside with Grant.

At about 6:30 p.m., Gillespie started his interview with Grant while Hume and Phelan waited outside in a different office. Gillespie advised Grant of his constitutional rights and his right to refuse to take a polygraph. Grant acknowledged both, signing the waiver for each.

Gillespie started the pre-interview portion of the test.

"Tell me about your actions on April 20," Gillespie said.

"I can't really remember," Grant said.

After a moment, Grant began sobbing.

"I saw two little boys walking down a trail and followed them," he said. "After a while, they parted. I approached one of them and told him to take off his clothes. He wouldn't do it, so I hit him in the face. He took off his clothes. I had the knife, and I plunged it into his chest two or three times while he was lying on the ground.

"A few minutes later," Grant continued, "the other boy came over. I tried to block his view of the first boy, but he saw him. I grabbed him and wrapped a piece of line around his neck and strangled him. I wrapped it several times and then tied a knot in it.

"After that, I took off his clothing and put him next to the first boy.

Seattle police polygraph operator Dewey Gillespie interviewed Grant before giving him the examination. Grant suddenly confessed to killing the boys, as well as Erickson and Zulauf. *Courtesy of the* Seattle Times.

"I remember they were both wearing rubber boots and jackets. I remember that one of the jackets was green.

"I covered their bodies with leaves and vines and then left. I threw the knife away before I left the woods."

Gillespie just sat there, not saying anything.

Finally, Grant said, "Oh God! Why did I do it? I like little boys!"

"Gary, are you willing to give a signed statement to the Renton detectives?" Gillespie asked.

"Yes, I'll do it," Grant said.

Detective Gillespie walked out of his office and went to the room where Hume and Phelan waited.

"Grant just confessed to me that he killed the two boys."

GRANT

Wally Hume and Jim Phelan were stunned. They thought Grant might be involved at some level, but they didn't expect this. John Chance was sitting in jail, already charged with these murders—ones he'd confessed to.

"John Chance was a nut," Hume said later. "He'd tell you anything you wanted to hear."

They brought Grant into an office and interviewed him. After reading him his rights, they questioned him about the murders.

"How far did you go in school?" Hume asked.

"Tenth grade," Grant answered.

"I walked to the Jack-in-the-Box restaurant on Sunset Boulevard in Renton. I wanted to see a girlfriend named Sonja."

"Is that where you went first?" Hume asked.

"Yes, to the Sunset Highway."

"About what time do you think you left?"

"About eleven."

"Were you alone at the time?" Hume asked.

"Yes."

"Was Sonja there?"

"No."

"Then where did you go?"

"To try to find some shoes," Grant said. "I went to Wigwam, and then I went to Sears, and then I went to Bazaar."

"Could you find any shoes to buy?"

"No."

"Okay, then where did you go?" Hume asked.

"All I can remember," Grant said, "is that I know I was up there looking for the shoes and I came out and I remember coming up behind the two boys."

"You said you fell in the river twice, is that right?" Hume interrupted.

"I fell in the river."

"Why did you go in the river? Are you a fisherman?"

"I just walked up there to see if anyone was fishing," Grant said.

"Did you actually fall in the river on two occasions?"

"Twice," Grant answered.

"Would that be up off Maple Valley Road?" Hume asked. "Is this where you first fell in the river?"

"Yes."

"Did you slip? Is that the way you fell in?"

"I was either bending over too far, slipped and lost my footing."

"Okay, then where did you go?" Hume continued. "Is that when you went up the hill?"

"I'm trying to tell you; I am on the river and the next part I can remember is coming up behind the two boys…"

The door to the room opened.

"Would you care for coffee, Gary?"

After a moment, Grant attempted again to confess.

"Okay, Gary," Hume said. "Going out to Maple Valley; could you take me to this place? How would you describe this area?"

"I was around the golf course," Grant said.

"Did you have the knife with you at that time?"

"Yeah," Grant said. "I had to have."

"And did you also have the cord with you, or rope or whatever?" Hume asked. "Where did you get that?"

"I found it on the tracks."

"How long do you think the rope you had was?"

"Two and a half to three feet."

"And you had the knife with you—the one with tape on the handle, right?"

"Yes."

"Okay, so you went up the Cedar River, and you slipped and fell headfirst and you got yourself all wet. Then where did you go?"

"Between the river and there it's just a blank spot. The next thing I can remember is coming up behind the boys," he said. "It's just a blank area there."

"Do you remember what time it was?"

"No."

Was this up on the hill above the Cedar River?"

"Yes."

"Were you walking?" Hume asked. "Were the boys walking?"

"Yes," Grant answered.

"Where were you walking—on a path, or down a hill, or on a level or what?"

"On a path."

"Was it a steep path?" Hume asked.

"It was level," Grant answered.

"Is there anything else about the area you could identify?"

"The river was on my right, down below me."

"How old were the boys?" Hume asked. "How old did they look?"

"They looked about five or six," Grant said.

At that point, the tape the detectives had been recording Grant's statement on ended. They changed the tape, but incredibly, the first sixty-five feet of tape did not record. That included the entire part of the recording during which Grant explicitly described murdering the boys. Despite Grant's repeated attempts to do so, he was interrupted by the detectives insisting on background information first.

Grant provided and signed a written statement detailing those facts.

After slipping into the river near Maplewood Golf Course, I remember coming up behind two boys on a hill about the Cedar River. This hill would be to the right of the Cedar River as you walk southeast from Renton. There were a lot of trees around, and I began walking northwest of the Cedar River quite a ways. To my right were two boys who looked about five to six years old. The boys had medium length hair. One boy had brown hair, and I can't remember if the other boy's hair was brown or lighter. Both boys were wearing jackets; both had rubber boots that were dark in color. One set of boots had a red band around the top of them. One boy's jacket seemed to be greenish.

I followed the boys for about a quarter mile. We went down a hill to a bog to my left. I followed the boys through the bog. They had not seen me at this time. I went up the side of the hill about one-half the way, and the two boys stopped at a small level area. I stayed out of sight and watched them for a minute. The two boys broke apart, and one stayed where he stopped. I then walked up to the boy who had stopped. I pulled the knife out of my pocket and showed it to the boy and told this boy to take off his clothes. He tried to run away, and I grabbed him, and this time, he took off all his clothes but his pants. I hit him in the face, and then I forced him to the ground and [stabbed him twice] *in the chest.*

At this time, I could hear the [other] *boy walking back through the woods. I left the boy I stabbed on the ground and backed away. When the other boy saw what happened to* [the other boy], *he was standing with his back to me. I was hiding behind the brush in a bend in a hill.*

I walked up to the [other boy] *with the cord in my hand. The cord had a loop in one end that I put around his neck. I pulled the loop tight around his neck. I then took the remainder of the rope and wrapped it around the boy's neck. After doing this to the second boy, I removed this boy's boots, coat, pants, and underpants,* [maybe] *and left on his shirt.*

It crossed my mind to feel the boy's privates, but I didn't. I left the cord around the boy's neck, and I threw the knife away in the woods. I then threw some brush and ferns on the boys. This covered them, but not their heads.

At this point, the recording continued with Wally Hume. Grant was discussing the route by which he fled the scene.

"Same direction, away from the hill?" Hume asked. "Would that be from the way you approached or what?"

"That would be toward the river," Grant answered.

"Okay, then what did you do, Gary, at that point?"

"I took off."

"Did you run?"

"Yeah."

"Which way did you run?" Hume asked. "Up the hill? Down the hill?"

"I ran down alongside it toward Renton," Grant answered.

"Did you go down to the railroad tracks on the Cedar River?"

"Yeah."

"Is that when you fell in the river again?"

"No," Grant said. "I came out by the railroad where it crosses the river."

"The railroad bridge there?"

"Yeah."

"Okay, then what did you do?" Hume asked. "Did you cross the river on the bridge or what?"

"No, I walked back toward Renton on the railroad tracks."

"Was that back of Renton?"

"Yeah," Grant said. "I went back down, and I thought I saw something in the water—sand or something."

"While walking in Renton, you again went to the Cedar River?"

"Yes."

"Did you run across it when you did this or not? You thought you saw something floating in the river."

"I thought I saw something in the water. I did not know quite what. I went down the bank to find out; saw it was some paper or something hanging on a branch under the water, and when I turned around to go back up the bank, I slipped and fell backward into the water."

"Okay," Hume continued, "you fell backward and got all wet. Then what did you do?"

"I floated down the river about forty feet."

"Then what did you do?"

"I tried to get a hold of something, and my foot caught onto a rock or something and I got a chance to get ahold of the bank, and I climbed out and then went over to Serve-U to call my mom to find out if my dad was awake so he could come down and pick me up."

After killing Lyons and Andrews, Grant crossed the Cedar River by walking across this trestle on his way to Frankie's Serve-U. *Photo by Cloyd Steiger.*

"The Serve-U Market is on Park Street, right?" Hume asked.

"I guess it is."

"What did your mother say?"

"She said he was asleep."

"Did you get a ride?"

"No," Grant answered.

"When you mentioned you hit one of the boys in the face, was that the first boy or the second boy?"

"That was the first boy."

"What did you hit him with, your fist?"

"Yeah," Grant said.

"How come you happened to be up in that area? Were you just wandering around for no apparent reason, or did you actually have some reason for going up in that area?"

"I don't know."

"Do you walk around like this a lot?"

"Yeah."

"So, it would not necessarily be unusual for you to walk around in the woods like this, is that right?" Hume asked, likely not realizing how important this question would later become.

"Do you walk in this area, particularly? Have you ever been around in that area before?"

"No."

At the end of the interview, Hume stepped out of the room. He called Pat Harber, the chief criminal deputy of the King County Prosecutor's Office, to update her on developments in the case. Harber was very concerned; she had another man in custody, already charged with the murders.

At 9:20 p.m., Seattle detective Dewey Gillespie approached Wally Hume. "Let me talk to Gary again."

He led Grant back into the polygraph room.

"I'd like to speak with you about a different crime," Gillespie said. "It involves a girl, a riverbank and a shoestring."

Grant thought for a moment and then said, "Was she stabbed in the back? Was it at night? Did she have long black hair?"

Gillespie didn't answer the questions. Finally, he said, "Why don't you tell me what you remember about the incident."

"I was behind a girl," Grant started. "I stabbed her in the back with a hunting knife. The knife had a blade about six inches long and about an inch and a half wide.

"After stabbing the girl, I took the shoestrings from her shoes and tied them together, and then I wrapped them around her neck."

"Did you take off her clothes?" Gillespie asked.

"I don't remember. I know she was wearing jeans, stockings and a ski-type jacket.

"After I stabbed her," he continued, "I dragged her over to some stickers and left her lying on her back.

"Before I left, I saw a man and woman walking toward Renton across the bridge. The man was dressed like a businessman, and the woman wore a white or yellow dress. When I saw them, I took off up to the railroad tracks. I threw the knife into some stickers near a fence."

Suddenly, Grant spontaneously talked about another murder. "She was laying on her back in some woods. There was no knife. I came up behind her; she didn't notice me. I hit her with something I had in my hand. I hit her in the back of the head. She was wearing a green-looking old army jacket and jeans. I just dazed her with a rock, and she stumbled forward. She started to say something. I grabbed her around the neck and choked her until she was dead.

"After I choked her, I heard some kids nearby, so I took off running up a trail. I don't remember where it was. She had dark reddish-brown hair."

Gillespie walked back out of his office to meet the Renton detectives.

"Gary just confessed to killing two girls," Dewey said to the incredulous detectives.

He showed them his notes of what Grant said. Hume recognized the first case as the murder of Carol Erickson, which had happened almost two years earlier.

Hume and Phelan brought Grant back in to interview him about the Erickson murder.

"Gary, we'd like to talk to you about what you said to Detective Gillespie. Are you willing to speak with us about that?" Hume asked.

"Yeah, I'll talk," he said. "I want to get this all out of me."

"Tell us what happened with the first girl you spoke about."

"Sometime before Christmas 1969, I saw a girl walking along the river on the left-hand side as it flowed toward the Renton Airport," Grant said. "This girl was walking toward the airport and carried a folder of some type in her arm."

"What was she wearing?" they asked.

"She was wearing blue jeans, I think a blue jacket, sort of leather tie-on shoes and a sweater.

"I first noticed her as she was approaching the railroad tracks. I walked along behind her for about ten to twelve feet. I was carrying a knife in my coat pocket."

"What did the knife look like?"

"I would describe it as having a straight blade. It had some sort of handle.

"I walked up behind her," Grant continued, "and thrust the knife into her back. I pulled it out and dropped it on the ground. She fell backward onto her back. I undid her shoelaces—both shoelaces—and tied them into a knot, but I don't remember what kind.

"I dragged her by the hands up to some stickers. I went back to get the knife when I noticed two people, a man and a woman, coming across the bridge. It was nighttime; just after dark."

"What were you wearing?"

"At the time I was wearing a green jacket, short with a zipper. I don't remember what else I was wearing that night."

"What did you do next?"

"I saw this man and woman and thought they might see me, so I picked up the knife and ran up the back to the railroad tracks, toward the airport. I reached the track and started walking toward Boeing. I took the knife and threw it into some stickers. These stickers were on the right-hand side as I was walking toward Boeing between the tracks and a wire fence. I don't think I'd walked too far before I threw the knife."

"What do you remember about the [second] girl?"

"She was a pretty girl. I think she was around seventeen or eighteen years old. Darker-colored hair, long.

"I can picture her vividly laying on her back, arms over her head. Her shoes were off. One arm of the coat had slipped off her arm. This happened when I went to pull her back. This was the right-hand side as I pulled her back."

"Did you take her clothes off?"

"I can see her sweater. I don't remember touching her clothes in any way."

"What happened then?"

"It was at that time that I got the knife and left. I don't remember anything about touching her clothes or sexually. I guess I could have blacked out for a while."

"What happened after that?"

"I was walking on the tracks. I can remember vaguely walking through the Boeing area after this happened.

"I don't know why I do these things," Grant continued. "I'm telling you the truth. There's nothing else I can tell you at this time; I may be able to later on."

Hume and Phelan didn't know much about the second girl Grant admitted to killing, but they thought it might be a case being investigated by the King County sheriff. That girl's name was Zulauf.

At about eleven o'clock that evening, Hume called the radio room of the sheriff's office. They put him in touch with Sergeant George Helland. Helland told Hume he was on his way to Seattle police headquarters. He arrived at about 12:15 a.m.

Hume introduced Grant to Helland. Helland asked Hume to sit in on the interview.

"How old are you, Gary?" Helland asked.

"I'm nineteen," Grant answered.

Helland went over Grant's rights.

"Can you tell us what year [Zulauf's murder] was again, Gary?" Helland asked.

"No," Grant answered.

"How long ago was it, approximately?"

"I don't know. Um…"

"Well let's try to establish it in months," Helland said. "We can go back. Let's go back to Christmastime of the end of the year. Was it before then?"

"I don't know," Grant said.

"Let's see, well you tell me a little bit about it and see if we can establish some dates. This is somewhat important, not altogether important, but somewhat important. Let's see if we can establish a date. You tell me about what happened. This is in regard to a young girl with dark hair, and she was hit in the back of the head. Let's start with that one."

"Well, I said earlier," Grant said, "that I came down there, it was in the woods, and I saw her ahead of me, and I came up behind her, and she didn't see me, and I had a rock in my hand. I struck her on the back of the head. She fell down, started to say something, and I grabbed her around the throat and choked her until she was dead, and about that time, I heard some kids' voices around me, I didn't know where. It sounded like they were coming my way, so I took off."

"I see," Helland replied. "It would be necessary for you to tell me some more particulars and some more details. I know which case you're talking about, but after that much time has passed, it would be necessary for you to tell me a little more about the physical actions that you took other than striking her in the back of the head and holding her throat. What did you use on her throat?"

"Just my hand."

"Just your hands. Until she was dead."

"Yes."

"What else can you tell me after that, after she was down on the ground? Other things that happened to her, I would assume you could tell me what they were?"

"I don't know; I know I choked her until she was dead, and I heard the kids' voices."

"And which position did you leave her?" Helland asked.

"She was lying on her back."

"Okay, do you remember which direction her head was facing, for instance?"

"It was downhill," Grant answered. "Clear on sort of a slanted slope and it was downhill.

"Describe her clothing to me when you first seen her."

"Oh, gads. She had sort of a, it seemed to me, an army jacket of some sort or service jacket she had. I'm not positive. I think it was blue jeans she had on, and she had some dark shoes."

"Did she have a shirt of any kind or a blouse, do you recall?"

"I don't know. The coat was together, it wasn't apart."

"Can you tell me what was in your mind or what your thoughts were at the time that you come up behind her?"

"I don't really know," Grant said.

"Tell me about her hair color and length."

"It was sort of a reddish-brown. It came down just about to her shoulders, and it was curly."

"What did she say to you, Gary, if anything? What did she say?"

"Nothing, really. I mean, to my memory, she started to say something, and that's when I grabbed her around the throat."

"How did you happen to be in the area?"

"I don't know."

"Could you take me to that area today or tomorrow? The same spot?"

"No, 'cause I don't know where it was."

"How did you leave? Can you tell me how you left from there?"

"I left on a trail," Grant said. "There was a trail going up a hill, winding up the side of the hill."

"What did it come out at when you got to the top?" Helland asked.

"I don't know. I don't remember."

"Do you remember what you seen when you got out of wherever you were at the top of the hill?"

"No. I remember running on the trail, and that's it."

"Do you remember her shoes? You said they were dark in color. Did you remove her shoes?"

"No, I did not," Grant answered, before adding, "Well, I can't really say that either 'cause I just don't…"

"You know by my hesitation, there is more to it than that, than the way you explained to me, so I would hope that you would just go ahead and say everything you did, down to the last item."

"I can't. I can't really say that I really didn't, and I don't think—I can't really say that I did because I don't know."

"It's only fair to you that I not suggest anything other than what you tell me, so all in your fairness and I want to be fair to you, because you faced this responsibility this evening and this past day, and I just, I want to be completely fair with you, so this is why I'm not suggesting anything. I'm letting you tell me, but I'm telling you there is more description, and I would hope that you can recall this for me."

"I know after I choked her," Grant said, "that I realized she was dead, that I heard some kids' voices, where they were coming from, I don't know, but it seemed like they were coming in my area, coming toward me.

"Remember, I just got up, sort of looked around and took off up the trail. Where I came out at, I don't know. Remember being on the trail, and I can't say that I did any more to her. I can't say I did, and I can't say I didn't. I don't know."

"What time of the day was it? This would be quite important to recall."

"Seemed like the sun was out. It was sort of cloudish like it was later in the afternoon.

"About what time would you fix it at, just if you don't remember? Approximately what time?"

"Somewhere around three to four in the afternoon."

"Okay," Helland said. "Did she resist you or fight back?"

"Yes," Grant answered.

"Did she cause you any damage?"

"No."

At this point, Helland had to be concerned. Grant was telling him the basic facts of the case, but he might have heard those facts anecdotally or read them in the paper. Helland had to get Grant to tell him something only the killer would know to confirm this wasn't a false confession.

"I've got to bring it up again. There are still some things I feel you may have left out, Gary, and without me telling you what they are, I want to know what you did with this girl after she was dead, or at least while she was partly unconscious or while she was dead. There are some steps in your memory or in your recall that I have to know. Now I know the answers, but I want you to tell me without my suggesting them, all in fairness to you. This is what I'm interested in, so let's…you struck her with a rock that was in your hand or an object that was in your hand. You felt that it was a rock. Am I correct?"

"Yes."

"Directly in the middle of the head, or was it on the back of the head, or was it on top of the head, or…?"

"I know it was on the head. I don't know exactly where."

"Her back was to you?"

"Yes."

"Which way did she fall?"

"She fell to her knees toward downhill, toward the downhill slope."

"Then what did you do?"

"And then I grabbed her around the throat. I came up behind her and grabbed her around the throat, and she started to say something."

"Did she see your face? Or were you behind her?"

"She saw my face because when she hit the ground, and I grabbed her, she swung around on me. She saw me."

"Then what did you do?"

"I kept choking her."

"There are still further steps. You must understand."

"I know."

"You say she was wearing an army-type jacket with blue jeans."

"Some sort of, yeah."

"It was army colored?"

"I'm not positive."

"Well, this is what I thought what you said to me."

"I'm not positive," Grant said, appearing to talk about something other than the color of her coat. "But I may have done something in that time. If I did, I wish I knew."

"I'm a little concerned about the location of her wristwatch," Helland said. "Can you help me out there?"

"Wristwatch?" Grant said.

"Umm hum."

"Don't remember any wristwatch."

"Do you recall if she was wearing earrings?"

"No. She may have been. I just don't know."

"Can you tell me the color of her clothing under her coat?" Helland asked, still trying to find any small piece of information that would corroborate that Grant was actually there.

"No."

"If you thought real hard, do you think you could?"

"I don't know."

"You see," Helland pressed, "certain physical actions took place right after she was killed, and we know this by certain bloodstains. I just want you to tell me in your own words if you will. It would have happened between the time you struck her with the rock until the time you left. I know you can tell me, Gary, but I don't want you to be embarrassed. I just want you to tell me the best way."

"No," Grant replied. "I want it to come out. If I did something wrong, I want it to come out. I don't want to hold it in myself anymore."

"Did you remove her clothing?"

"I don't know. I can't say whether I did or not."

"Tell me a little bit about the area—where she fell or where you left her. Was it—did she fall down the same place you left her, or did you have to move her from that place to another?

"No, I left her where she fell down at."

"Was the area extremely brushy and a lot of branches right there, or was it relatively clear?"

"It was relatively clear in that area where she was laying. Around there, there was lots of brush."

"Did you see anything unusual right on that spot that you can recall? Any strange objects that didn't belong in the woods or that was just laying nearby?"

"No, not that I can remember anything."

"Do you remember touching her with your hands or anything other than your hands after she was dead?"

"No, I can't recall anything, but I just don't know. I may have."

"Did you hit her in the mouth?"

"I can't remember if I did or not."

"How tall was she, Gary?"

"Oh, about five feet."

"She was a rather small girl?"

"Yes."

"How old do you think she was?"

"About fifteen or sixteen," Grant said in the calm tone he'd used throughout the conversation, describing the snuffing out of innocent life as if recounting a weather forecast.

"What was her physical stature? Was she a heavy girl, medium build, skinny? How would you describe her?"

"Medium build."

"About medium, huh? Was she well developed for her age?"

"I didn't pay attention to that."

"Had you ever seen her before?"

"No."

"Do you recall the area you were in or how you got there?"

"Up to where I saw her in front of me, I don't remember any other time of going there, how I got there or, other than starting to leave on the trail, where I went from there."

"Were you driving a car that day?"

"I don't know if I was or not."

"Do you recall," Helland said, "now that we've talked about it for a little bit, how long ago it was, what month it might have been in?"

"No," Grant replied.

"Was it over two years ago?"

"I don't know."

"Was it last month?"

"I don't know, I have no idea."

Helland must have been getting frustrated. Was this guy just trying to confess to any crime mentioned? He needed to get information only the killer would know.

"Why is it that you can remember so many good parts, Gary, and then— you know, I should say not good parts, but parts that are important—and yet some of the other parts you don't recall?

"Which direction was the sound of the children coming from as they were getting closer to you? Was it behind you or in front of you? Where did the voices sound like they were coming from?"

"I really didn't know. I heard them. They sounded like they were getting closer. I really didn't know what direction or anything."

"How many voices did it appear to be?"

"Oh, it sounded like a group of kids. I wouldn't really know how many in number or anything. I know there was more than one voice."

"I think we're thinking about the same girl, Gary. I've got a case similar to this, but for your own benefit I'd like to make sure, and that's why I'm trying to draw out every little minute detail."

"I know. I'd tell you if I knew."

"I could suggest every little detail to you," Helland added. "I know the case inside and out. But it wouldn't be fair to you if I did that."

"No."

"I would want you to remember each and every little thing, and this is the way you're going to unload it. This is the way you're going to release your mind from the fullness and pressure you've had for these past months or however long. It's been weighing on you for quite a while I'd imagine."

"Well, that's just it," Grant replied. "I didn't know about what I'd done until this deal came up. I didn't know about any of it. I heard about the little kids. I told my dad I wanted to go up and help look for them.

"And I didn't know anything about what I'd done."

"I understand," Helland said. "Well, to get back to this one, if I told you that her clothing had been removed entirely, would that help you recall any?

"There's been a pattern, Gary, in each of the cases where you've injured someone that you've taken their clothing off or portions of their clothing."

"The two little kids, yes."

"How about the girls, though?"

"On some points," Grant said, "I just can't remember if I did or not. I just come to one point, and I'm just 'bam!' right to another point and I…"

"Okay, if I give you a piece of paper would you be able to draw me a sketch of the area as you recall it, as you recall the area where you came upon her, where you struck her, where you strangled her and choked her, can you tell me that? Can you give me something about the curve of the land or what's a hill and what's not a hill and what's trees?"

"Yes," Grant said. "I'll tell you the basic area of the land around it."

"Okay, that's fair enough. You take my pen. Let's make it a stick-body in what you think is the direction she was facing, and then we'll go on and build the terrain around. In the direction that you think you left her arms and legs and head; which direction were they facing? We don't care what's north now, we'll establish that later."

Grant took the pen and paper and began drawing.

"The arms," Grant said, "sort of bent like that."

"Where would the head be?"

"Right here," Grant said, drawing on the paper.

"Okay, and the other arm?"

"Laying out to the side," Grant said, drawing again.

Helland was finally getting specific information from Grant about the scene.

"Okay, and the left leg, "he said. "Apparently, you're seeing a picture just as you left, right?

"Yes."

"Which way were you standing at this time?"

"I'm standing, looking this way," Grant said, gesturing to the sketch.

"Just make an X about where you're standing at about the time you left."

Grant complied.

"Okay, now that's the other leg," Helland said. "Okay, how would you describe that?"

"This part of her was slightly turned to her side, and the leg was bent underneath the other one," Grant said, describing the scene with tremendous specificity now. "Then it leveled out to where she was laying on her back up here."

"Okay, and it was downhill, right? Her head was downhill? Did you state that earlier?"

"Yes."

"Okay, where was the hill from here?"

"There was one; some sort of gulley. There was one rise across here," Grant said, again gesturing to the sketch.

"Okay, and was there any other ones?"

"And then, the one I started up sort of over in here."

"Okay, and what laid back in that direction? Was it flat or gulley or…?"

"No, it was bank there."

"It went upward, okay, and what happened when you went here?"

"That seemed to be kind of sloping gulley which sort of sharpened out in here."

"Sharpened out; do you mean narrowed down?"

"To a V. Here, it went to a V," again, pointing to the sketch.

"Just make the lines you would indicate that it would narrow to a V. Whatever lines that you'd like to make it to do so.

"And there it is a bank; would you write the word *bank* for me?"

"Let's see," Grant said. "Well, these were two banks here."

Helland went through the sketch, having Grant label various landmarks and terrain areas, and asked him to initial the X he'd marked indicating his position.

"Now show me the direction that you were traveling. Make a dotted line to show your traveling."

"You mean?"

"The path you took."

"Leaving?"

"No, following her and coming up behind her. Do you recall?"

"The only thing I can recall," Grant said, "is straight behind her, coming in. Straight in."

"Which way did you leave? To the best of your recollection."

"I left in this direction," Grant said, gesturing to the sketch. "Off this way. There was a trail in here."

"Okay," Helland said. "I think I've got a better picture, but I think I've helped you develop a better picture too, Gary, in as much as you remember the position of her arms. You remember the direction of her head that she was facing downhill, that her legs were, one was up and spread apart, the other one somewhat straighter, down from her body, and that they possibly crossed at the ankles. This left a deep impression in your mind, am I correct?"

"Yes."

"Okay, you could see her face looking straight up at the time you left?"

"Well, it was off at a slant."

"Which way was it facing?"

"This way here," again, gesturing to the sketch.

"So now you remember real well. Now I would want you to really try for me and for yourself to tell me where her clothes were at this time. This isn't much of a big hurdle to get over, Gary, because you've told me every step of the way. We're just right down to the clothes."

"At that time, that I stood there and looked at her, her clothes were on her. She was dressed."

"Could you have returned afterward?"

"I could have. I can't say whether I did or not; I just don't know. I wish I did."

"Have you been able to think in that short intermission?"

"Yeah, but I see up to that point and then no further. It just…"

"What was the last point? Is that where you had your hands around her throat?"

"Yes."

"Okay, was she laying on the ground when you did this or was she standing up?"

"She was laying on the ground."

"Flat down on her face, or on her back?"

"On her back."

"Okay, what were you doing? What were your positions—standing, kneeling?"

"Kneeling."

"Did she have anything in her hands?"

"No."

"What did you do when you let loose with your hands?"

"I let loose with my hands," Grant said, "stood up, I heard kids' voices, I couldn't tell where they were coming from, but it sounded like they were coming in my direction, so I went back up and around and left. I started going up the trail, then I can't remember anymore."

Helland questioned Grant more, trying to tie down a location or approximate time this event occurred, but Grant continued to insist he had no idea. Grant also denied knowledge of what he hit Joanne with, though he thought it was probably a rock. He claimed he could not describe the rock, whether it was round or sharp, where he got it or any other details.

"Did you run up behind her," Helland asked, "or walk up behind her?"

"I walked."

"Which hand did you hold the rock in?"

"My right."

"She fell forward all the way to her face at that time?"

"No, she fell to her knees."

"Just stunned, right?"

"Yeah."

"Then what did you see next or do next?"

"After I hit her," Grant said, "and she went to her knees, I started going for her, and she started to say something or scream, and I grabbed her around the throat."

"What did you do with the rock?"

"I don't know. I must have dropped it."

"What did her body do when you were choking her, Gary?"

"Her back was arching, and her hands and arms were trying to push me away."

"Then what did you do?"

"I kept choking her until there was no more movement. Then I let go of her. She wasn't breathing."

"Did you have any thoughts of removing her clothes at the time?"

"I don't know if I did or didn't."

"Did you notice any blood?"

"No."

"It was daylight now, wasn't it?"

"Yes."

The interview ended at 2:10 a.m.

The Renton detectives had a problem in how to deal with Grant. They already had John Chance formally charged with the murders of Lyons and Andrews. He was scheduled to be arraigned in the case in two days. They couldn't also book Grant with the killings with no information he was with Chance.

They decided to book him for material witness to murder. That would give them some time to sort things out.

Unbeknownst to the Renton detectives at the time, the rooms that both John Chance and, later, Gary Grant were placed in had listening and recording devices installed by Captain William Frazee. Both men spoke to their attorneys in those rooms, and their conversations were recorded. Not only were the recordings of communications without a court order illegal in the state of Washington, but the tapes of conversations with their attorneys also threatened the entire case. It was conceivable that because of these recordings, a known serial killer could walk free.

When prosecutors learned of the recordings, they went into serious damage control mode.

FOLLOW-UP

While Chance entered the not guilty plea, Gary Gene Grant sat in the Renton City Jail as a material witness to murder after having confessed in detail to the same murders with which Chance had been charged, as well as the deaths of Carol Erickson and Joanne Zulauf.

In the meantime, Renton detectives went about investigating Grant more thoroughly.

On May 4, Detective Hubner interviewed Norma Flister, who worked as a clerk at Frankie's Serve-U grocery store, where Grant earlier had told detectives he went after killing Lyons and Andrews and falling in the Cedar River a second time.

"When I was first asked if anything unusual had happened in the store on the day school was out," Flister said, "I said I couldn't think of anything until you asked if I remember a wet customer. Then I remembered a young man being wet on that day.

"I first saw him standing by check stand one," she continued. "I was stocking the candy section when I saw him. He was about nineteen to twenty years old. I'm about five feet one. I think he was probably about five eight or five nine. He wasn't heavy-set."

"How would you describe his build?" Hubner asked.

"He was medium. He certainly wasn't heavy-set."

"Do you remember how he was dressed?"

"I don't remember. I just remember he was wearing casual clothing. By that I mean, he wasn't wearing a suit and a tie."

Gary Grant was soaking wet when he walked into Frankie's Serve-U after murdering Lyons and Andrews. The clerk there later remembered him. *Photo by Cloyd Steiger.*

"When he approached the check stand, I saw that he was wet.

"You're wet,' I said to him. 'I fell in the river,' he told me. 'You must be cold,' I said. 'I'm freezing,' he said.

"He purchased something," Flister continued, "but I don't remember what. He handed me a wet one-dollar bill. I handed him his change, and when I did, I touched his hand. It was very cold. He walked out the front door.

"In a couple minutes, he walked back in and came back to the check stand area. He asked for change to use the payphone. He said something about calling someone to get him. He also asked for a book of matches. I went back to work and didn't give him any more thought."

"Do you know what time he came in?" Hubner asked.

"Well," Flister said, "on that day, I took my lunch at four in the afternoon. I know it was before I went to lunch. I commented to the owner that the kids were out of school, and we were probably going to be bugged by them all day."

Hubner showed her a photo montage consisting of seven photographs of young men.

"I know I've seen this young man before," Flister said, holding up photo number four. "I can't say if this is the man who came in that day, but I've seen him before."

Photo number four was of Gary Gene Grant.

Chief criminal deputy prosecutor David Boehner was riding in a car with two Renton detectives when they spoke about conversations Grant had with this attorney. Boehner was shocked. Based on the discussion, it became evident that those conversations had been recorded. That was not only shocking and illegal, but it also threatened the case itself.

He found that the room Grant and his attorney were in had been wired for recording by Renton police chief of detectives William Frazee without anyone noticing.

The King County Prosecutor's Office notified both Grant and Chance's attorneys of the unlawful recordings of their clients. No one from the prosecutor's office had listened to the recordings—something that would prove crucial in court hearings about the tapes later.

On May 10, prosecutors had a bombshell announcement: they were dismissing the charges against John Arthur Chance, who'd spent more than a week in custody, accused of murders he did not commit. They also announced charges against Gary Gene Grant of murder in the first degree for the deaths of Carol Erickson, Joanne Zulauf, Bradley Lyons and Scott Andrews. Elected prosecutor Christopher Bayley later announced he would seek the death penalty against Grant for the murders.

Additionally, the prosecutor's office announced criminal charges of unlawful electronic interception of a conversation against Renton police captain William Frazee, a gross misdemeanor carrying the possibility of a year in jail. Frazee was immediately put on leave from the Renton Police Department as a result of the charges. A special prosecutor from the state attorney general's office was brought in to handle that case.

Grant's attorneys immediately filed a motion to dismiss the charges against him because of the unlawful recordings.

Soon after charging, the case was assigned to King County Superior Court judge David Soukup, a young but well-respected judge in King County. He had the experience and demeanor to tread the minefield that was this case carefully.

While prosecutors prepared to respond to Grant's attorneys' motion to dismiss, they also continued to prepare the case for trial.

On May 17, Grant had his first psychiatric evaluation by Dr. George Harris, which took place in the King County Jail. Dr. Harris described Grant as comfortable during the four-hour session. He appeared to be aware of the trouble he was in and the charges he faced.

"Have you ever been seen by a psychiatrist before?" Harris asked.

"When I stayed with my sister Penny in Oregon for about three or four months, I was in counseling at Saint Helens."

Grant explained that there were problems when he stayed with his sister, including her "downgrading" his mother about her drinking and that his sister favored her three young sons over him.

He told Harris that he returned to the Seattle area around Christmas 1968. He told Harris he faltered in high school and then joined the navy.

Christopher Bayley was the newly elected King County prosecutor when Gary Grant was arrested. *Courtesy of Christopher Bayley.*

"I was discharged two months later," he said. "I had a sadistic CO named Furrer. He would beat me up. I also got a reputation for being a mamma's boy. The navy played dirty tricks on me. I had a drug infraction, and they stuck me in the stockade with the dopers. I talked to a chaplain, and they eventually discharged me."

Grant talked about his life after the navy.

"I really didn't do much. I drove for a Phillips gas station for about a month. I drove a truck for my neighbors for about three months and worked on and off at Maplewood Golf Course.

"I was engaged to my girlfriend, Bev, until just after my discharge. My father told me he and my mom didn't like her, and it was either her or them.

"I spend a lot of time walking in the woods," Grant told Harris. "I also help my friends work on small engines."

"Tell me about your early life," Harris said.

"When I was small, my parents bought a boat," Grant said. "We lived on it for about seven years. My parents separated a few times then. My dad made bad business decisions, and my mom had a drinking problem."

Earlier, Harris had interviewed Grant's father. Glen Grant told Harris that his wife, Penny, would become abusive to him when she was drunk, and he would leave for a few weeks at a time. He estimated he was gone 30 percent of the time.

"When my mom drank," Grant told Harris, "she would get angry and throw dishes. One time she whirled around on me and had a knife in her hand."

Harris asked Grant if he ever masturbated.

"No," Grant said.

"Wasn't there a time when you masturbated on a picture about a murder in a detective magazine?"

"I may have," Grant said.

Harris pressed him on that. "Don't you think you'd be sure one way or the other about something like that?"

Grant was "nonplussed" by this, Harris later reported.

Grant described three times that he remembered being in a dissociative state.

"One time, when I was in the ninth grade, I was modeling clay. Suddenly, everything was quiet. I could see other people moving around and things, and I could hear my own voice, but I couldn't hear anything else. People seemed to look right through me. The next thing I remember was being at home."

He described another instance like that.

"My mom told me that Oliver [a family friend] was killed in a car accident. I passed out. I was aware of what was going on around me but couldn't hear anything.

"Another time, I was in the stockade in the navy. I escaped and was arrested an hour and a half later. I don't remember that at all."

When Harris asked him about the killings he was accused of, Grant would close his eyes and bow his head. He told Harris that he could see "the killing taking place" but never said that he saw himself doing it.

"I see a hand with a rock hitting a girl on the side of the head," Grant said. "I see a knife going into a girl's back. I see a boy getting undressed, and I see a knife going into his chest. I see a hand holding a length of twine wrapping around a boy's neck and being choked."

As Harris asked questions about the incidents, Grant was able to go forward and backward through the events smoothly.

"I saw a knife thrown into some bushes by a fence," Grant said.

"At about one to two o'clock that day," Grant said, this time with his eyes open and communicating normally, "I was looking at a fish and fell in the river. I called my mother about two-fifteen and was home by three o'clock."

As Grant spoke of the murders, he added that it was "wrong to kill." He said he realized that stabbing a person could kill them. He had no impulses or feelings at "seeing" this done. He had "no feeling at all."

Harris noted that Grant was in good contact with his environment and situation. He became agitated when recounting his "visions" of the killings, of which he declared his innocence. He appeared indifferent to his predicament. "I'll probably go to Canada with my folks when this is over," Grant told Harris.

Harris noted that there was "no evidence of thought disorder, delusions, or hallucinations."

Grant denied drug use to Harris, as well as any suicidal intent. He expressed disbelief that he could be charged with these crimes while offering no explanation as to his vivid visual images of the crimes themselves.

Dr. Harris opined that Grant was of borderline intelligence. Harris diagnosed Grant as dissociative reaction, with a rule out of psychomotor or other seizure problem.

Harris added that "in view of this client's rather clear recitation of the events of the killings themselves, I would say he had an adequate understanding of the acts and a moral appreciation of their wrongness.... He is qualified to stand trial."

Dr. Harris's contention that Grant was able to understand the wrongness of his actions was significant. The definition of legal insanity (as opposed to medical insanity) is the ability of the person to understand the difference between right and wrong at the time of the event. In Harris's opinion, Grant was legally sane at the time of the killings.

The detectives investigating Gary Grant wanted to learn more about who he was and his history. They began interviewing people he associated with. One of the acquaintances was Cheri Kramer.

"I met Gary at a beach party in the summer of 1970," she told detectives. "I met him through a friend, Frank Piggott.

"I saw him a lot that summer. I hung out with Frank, and Gary was always there."

She told the detectives that she went to Renton Vocational College at the same time as Joanne Zulauf but didn't know her.

"I was at a house party at Frank's house on September 11, 1970. I saw Gary give Linda Loomis a watch. Well, I didn't actually see him give it to her, but she was showing it off, telling everyone that Gary gave it to her."

"Can you describe the watch?" the detectives asked, knowing that Joanne Zulauf's watch was missing.

"I don't remember much about the watch," she said. "Leslie DeRemer saw the watch too. She may remember more about it."

"How would you describe Gary?"

"He was kind of boring. Always talking about his troubles. He seemed really insecure and immature. He was shy around girls."

They tracked down Linda Loomis.

"I met Gary at the beach in the late spring of 1970," she said. "We went out the night we met. Three days later, he told me he loved me. We went steady from May until mid-October that year."

"Tell us about when you were with Gary."

"We went to his uncle's property out by Tiger Mountain," she said. "He had horses, so we'd go horseback riding."

"How did Gary get around?"

"Usually, he drove his dad's red GMC pickup."

She told the detectives about a time she went with Gary and another couple to a drive-in movie.

"He exposed himself to me. I told him off, and he didn't persist."

She described a fight she had with Grant in early September that year.

"We got into an argument. I started seeing another boy. Gary found out and seemed hurt by it."

She described the party that Cheri Kramer had told them about.

"It was September 26 [about four days after the Zulauf murder]. Gary and Frank had a party at Frank's house. During the party, Gary pulled a girl's watch out of his pocket and gave it to me. I asked where he got it, and he said it was secondhand.

"Everyone wondered how Gary got the watch; he didn't have a job. He'd told me in the past about all these big things he did. I'd asked him why he never seemed to get paid for any of it. When he gave me the watch, he said, 'See. I do get paid for the things I do.'"

"Did you ever see him with a knife?"

"He showed me a hunting knife once," she said. "I never saw it in a truck or car."

She described a time shortly after Joanne Zulauf's murder. "I tried to talk to Gary about it. He wouldn't talk about it. He just clammed up."

Linda told the detectives about the last time she was with Gary.

"In early April on a Friday night, I called Gary. My parents weren't home, and I was there with a girl I know. I called Gary and asked him if he wanted to come over. He did, and eventually, three other couples came over too.

"We were drinking green apple wine. At about nine o'clock, everyone else left, so just Gary and I were there. Gary told me he still loved me and wanted to go steady again. I told him I liked another boy. He was very put down by that."

Lastly, Linda told the detectives about the day Bradley Lyons and Scott Andrews were killed.

"Nancy Todd and I skipped school that day and went to Issaquah. I thought about calling Gary. Nancy said, 'Don't do it.'"

Sergeant George Helland traveled to Pierce, Idaho, where Joanne's parents had moved after her murder. He met with Virginia Thompson, Joanne's mother. He showed her the watch they had recovered from Linda Loomis.

"That's Joanne's watch," Mrs. Thompson said. "I recognize the type of band, the shape of the crystal, and the eight-sided case, the brand name and the safety chain. I bought it for her on April 26, 1969, at the Renton Gov-Mart Bazaar, three days before her birthday."

The band on the watch Helland showed her was broken. "The band wasn't broken the last time I saw it," Thompson said. "It was on Joanne's wrist the day she was murdered."

Nancy Myrick also spoke to detectives about Gary.

"I moved from Renton to Benton City [in eastern Washington, 240 miles away] in August of 1970. Before that, I hung out with Gary a lot."

She told the detectives she came back to Renton for a weekend at the end of April and the beginning of May 1971.

"I was at Gary's house the day he was arrested," she said. "But I didn't see him."

She told the detectives Gary liked kids and spoke with them all the time.

Shortly after Carol Erickson was murdered, Nancy spoke with Gary's mother, Penny. "It's such a terrible thing to happen to a young girl," Penny told her. Penny wouldn't allow Nancy to walk home alone at night; she made Gary walk her.

Beverly Anderson had known Gary since the summer of 1968. "Gary proposed to me in 1969," she said. "We were engaged until sometime in 1970. Gary got into an argument with his folks. They told him that I wouldn't fit in with the family. He took the ring back."

She recounted a conversation with him on the phone in the summer of 1969. "He sounded strange. I asked him about it. He said he took a hit of acid. He told me he was mad at someone. He said he was mad enough to kill a kid."

She spoke of a time Gary called her at work once in April 1971. "He called about ten in the evening. He told me he'd been up all night helping the police look for the two missing boys."

He showed up at her high school during lunch break a couple weeks later. He was reticent. He finally told her he'd been in a fight over her.

"He was always lying about everything," she told the detectives. "He'd tell me the same story over and over again, but it'd be different every time. Whenever I questioned him about the differences, he'd get mad."

"Some friends and I were starting a band," Arthur "Dean" Robinson told George Helland. "During the first few months, we weren't too organized. Our band was called the Midnight Express.

"That September, we were doing pretty well. We landed a gig at Pluto's in Renton. One of my friends approached Gary Grant about driving us to and from gigs. Gary said he would and offered to look for other gigs we could play.

"He drove us to Pluto's in an older red pickup truck. He dropped us off and said he had a date with a girl. He picked us up at midnight. As we were driving home, the subject of the Zulauf murder came up. We were saying we hoped the killer would be caught and hanged. We all felt sorry for her. My friend Dennis Kreider knew her. He said what a nice girl she was.

"Everyone was agreeing about what should be done with the killer. Everyone was agreeing, nodding heads," he said. "Except Gary. He didn't say a thing. He didn't look up at anybody. He just kept quiet.

"I didn't think anything of it at the time, but after I heard Gary was arrested for the murder, it reminded me how he acted strange."

PROSECUTION

Christopher Bayley was elected prosecutor for King County in November 1970. He took office in January 1971. Shortly after starting his term, Bayley tackled the problem of a corrupt group of officers on the Seattle Police Department taking bribes from taverns and gambling dens around the city. He spearheaded grand jury investigations into the matter, which would eventually send several officers to prison and clean up the Seattle Police Department.

When a notorious crime happened in King County, Bayley met with his top advisors, chief criminal deputy David Boehner and chief civil deputy Norm Maleng, to discuss the case. Maleng would later follow Bayley as the elected prosecutor and would serve decades in that role.

"I relied on their advice to determine how to handle the case," Bayley said.

Now Bayley had the Gary Grant prosecution to deal with. The case was complicated by the illegal recording of Grant speaking with his attorney that had been made by Captain Frazee of the Renton Police Department.

When Bayley heard about the recording, he was aghast. "The first thing," he later said upon learning of the recording, "was how shocking that this would happen, and the fact that the police department involved in doing this seemingly not understanding that it was illegal and would ruin the case."

It was crucial that Bayley separate his office from the recording. C. Kenneth Gross, an assistant state attorney general, represented the prosecution at Frazee's arraignment, during which Frazee pleaded not guilty to the charges.

Gross would represent the state, along with David Boehner, who would assist Gross in trying the case against Frazee.

Bayley brought on a special prosecutor to help with the Grant case. He chose Edmund Allen, a former assistant chief criminal deputy for the prosecutor's office who had recently become a private attorney. Bayley's office was treading through a minefield, and any mistake could result in a notorious killer of four people, including two children, walking free. Assisting Allen was a young deputy prosecutor, Michael DiJulio. "I was an old guy at that time," DiJulio said. "Most people left after two years." DiJulio would work for thirty-six years at the King County Prosecutor's Office before finally retiring.

At the time of the Grant trial, DiJulio was the father of small children.

"Getting past the unlawful recording of Grant was the big hurdle in the case," DiJulio said. "And getting the confessions in."

The prosecution team worked hard to convict Gary Grant of the murders. Elected prosecutor Christopher Bayley signed a photo for Edmund Allen expressing his appreciation. *Courtesy of Edmund Allen Jr.*

Gary Grant's lawyers were former King County prosecutors James Anderson and C.N. "Nick" Marshall. DiJulio recalled, "Nick Marshall put [Grant] on the stand in the pretrial hearing, as well as during the trial, trying to keep him [from getting] the death penalty."

The case would weigh heavily on Ed Allen. His son, Edmund Allen Jr., was six years old at the time, the same age as Lyons and Andrews. Allen, who died in 2018, frequently spoke to his son about the case over the years.

"The thing I remember most poignantly about that is the boys were six. It was 1971, and I was exactly six then. I remember my dad talking specifically about the boots those boys were wearing, black rain boots with a little red stripe around it," Allen Jr., himself an attorney and former King County prosecutor, said about the case. "I had those exact same boots. My dad told me how he was thinking about those boys and their parents, taking the boys out to do the same things we would do. That hit him hard.

"He talked to me about a lot of his cases," Allen continued. "Especially when I went to work for the prosecutor's office. He talked about the detective [*sic*] bugging the room. Not just of a conversation, but a privileged conversation with his attorney that jeopardized the whole case. They had to

Special prosecutor Edmund Allen was disturbed by the killing of Andrews and Lyons. He had children of his own, one of whom was the same age. *Courtesy of Edmund Allen Jr.*

insulate the prosecutor's office. I remember the term he used: 'they made us wash all the evidence' to keep a level of separation between the actual case and the recording.

"Gary Grant was a particularly evil and prominent name he spoke of. My dad loved trying that case—his last as a prosecutor."

Very early in the case, the defense made a motion that all statements made by Grant after he was taken from the trailer court be ruled as inadmissible and that his tennis shoes and clothing, taken by the detectives, also be thrown out. They claimed that the Renton detectives had picked Gary up under a ruse of getting him to "help with the investigation." Grant had only gone through the tenth grade in school and, according to his lawyers, was "of low intelligence." They described this as a "calculated and deliberate act" to deprive Grant of his right to an attorney.

The defense also wanted to tell the jury that John Chance had previously confessed to the crime, so Grant could not be guilty.

They also moved to have a separate trial for each murder. Jurors would be a lot more likely to convict if the defendant was accused of committing several murders. In their brief supporting the motion, they noted that the murders were "not closely connected in a point in time [ironically, one definition of serial murder], and that the proof to support each count was different from the others. Use of all the information in one trial would deprive Grant of a fair trial because of the cumulative evidence engendered by the totality of the evidence presented."

There is a court rule, 404B, in which crimes shown to have a common plan or scheme are admissible in evidence in the trial of other crimes. This, indeed, showed evidence of such a plan.

Judge David Soukup issued his ruling to the motion on September 28, 1971. "I feel written, and oral statements are admissible, up to and including the statement taken by Detective [sic] Helland," he began. "The statements were taken after that, after 9:00 AM on May 1, are inadmissible." That ruling suppressed any statements Grant made to Detective Dashnea as he drove him around the scene of the boys' murders.

Judge Soukup also ruled that the only recorded statement of Grant's that was admissible was the one taken by Helland.

"I think that the tennis shoes were voluntarily given by the defendant to the police," Soukup said. "There was no search or seizure of these items."

Soukup also admitted Grant's clothing, noting that it was taken incident to arrest. He added that Grant voluntarily discussed the knife with the detectives and went with them to the police station willingly, noting that Grant rode in the back seat of their unmarked police car while they rode in the front, the doors to the car were unlocked and Grant was not in handcuffs.

In a closed hearing on June 28, 1971, the defense moved to dismiss the charges entirely because Grant's rights had been violated when his conversation with his previous attorney was recorded by the Renton Police Department. They based the motion on an earlier ruling by the Washington Supreme Court, which had dismissed charges in another county for a similar recording. In that case, the court ruled that because of the recording, the prosecution had gained an advantage over the defense.

On June 30, Judge David Soukup denied the motion to dismiss.

Superior Court judge David Soukup had to walk a minefield of issues in the Grant case, or a known serial killer could have walked free. *Courtesy of the* Seattle Times.

"An innocent public should not be penalized because of an illegal act on the part of the police department," Soukup said in his ruling. He noted that Frazee had been criminally charged for his actions.

Addressing the previous case dismissed by the state supreme court, Soukup found that the facts in the two cases were different. In the dismissed case, the prosecutor listened to the recordings. In this case, the prosecutor's office went out of its way to avoid listening to them, even bringing in an assistant attorney general to handle the case, further insulating the office.

"The criminal statute that makes charging possible," Soukup said, "puts the penalty where it belongs, instead of on an innocent public."

The trial for the four murders started on August 12.

"During jury selection," Edmund Allen Jr. said, "My dad asked the prospective jurors if they'd seen the movie *Hang 'Em High*, with Clint Eastwood. The defense objected, saying, 'This is not a theatrical event,' but there was a mass-hanging scene in that movie, and the death penalty was by hanging in Washington. He wanted to make sure they weren't prejudiced by that."

Finally, a jury of ten men and two women was empaneled, and the trial began.

Wally Hume testified about him and Jim Phelan going to Grant's trailer and noticing that the soles of the shoes Grant was wearing looked very similar to imprints found at the scene of the Andrews and Lyons murder scene.

The trial of *State of Washington v. Gary Gene Grant* took place in the King County Courthouse in downtown Seattle. The prosecutor's office is also located in the building. *Courtesy of the City of Seattle Archives.*

Dewey Gillespie testified next to interviewing Grant before the polygraph examination. "I advised him of his rights," Gillespie said, "and he said he understood. He never refused to answer any question I asked him."

Grant claimed to have lapses in his memory, Gillespie told the jury, and then began to sob. He told Gillespie what happened during the crimes, starting with the boys.

"He said he followed two boys down a trail," Gillespie said. "He did not want them to see him. They separated, and he approached one of the boys, asking him to get undressed.

"When the boy refused, Grant hit him in the face. After he hit him, the boy undressed. Grant stabbed him in the chest two or three times.

"When the other boy came back," Gillespie continued, "Grant said he strangled him with a cord he had with him."

Gillespie testified about Grant telling him how he placed the boys' bodies side by side and then covered them with vines and leaves.

Gillespie said Grant sobbed and said, "God, why did I do it? I like little boys!"

Gillespie's testimony then shifted to his questioning Grant about the Erickson murder.

"I gave him the phrases 'a girl, a riverbank, a shoestring.'"

"Grant asked, 'Was she stabbed in the back? Did she have long black hair?'"

Gillespie testified that Grant described following her down a trail and stabbing her in the back with a knife.

"He said he couldn't recall removing her clothing but did remove shoestrings from her shoes and tied them around her neck. He said he pulled her over to some bushes and then threw the knife away as he was leaving the scene."

Grant then began describing the Joanne Zulauf murder.

"He said he saw her lying on her back in a wooded area. He approached her from behind with a rock and hit her on the head. She started to say something. He put his hands on her neck and choked her."

Virginia Thompson, Joanne Zulauf's mother, took the stand. She identified the watch in evidence as belonging to Joanne. She said it was the same watch that Renton detectives brought to her home in Idaho, where she and her husband moved after the murder, and asked her if she recognized it.

Prosecutor Michael DiJulio had told jurors in his opening statement that a female friend of Grant's said that Gary had given her the watch, saying, "See. I do get paid for the things I do."

Clyde Reed described to the jury how he searched the area where Joanne was last seen with his bloodhound, eventually finding her body in a ravine.

A friend of Grant's, Richard Krantz, testified that he was in the area of the Zulauf murder about twelve hours after it happened when he came across Gary Grant, soaking wet and walking in the rain. He stopped and gave Grant a ride to his home, some distance away. When he asked Grant why he was so far from home, Grant simply said, "I was taking a walk."

Next came the powerful testimony of the mothers of Scott Andrews and Bradley Lyons. Both women wept during their testimony, describing seeing the boys playing on a dirt pile near their homes before walking into a wooded area nearby, never to see them alive again.

Scott Andrews's mother wept as she described the last time she saw her son. "He was laughing," she said. "He seemed so happy."

Dr. Gale Wilson testified about his findings from the autopsies of each victim, describing their last moments and what caused their deaths.

Kay Sweeney, from the Seattle Police Crime Lab, testified about the shoe print found at the scene of the boys' murder and his comparison to Grant's tennis shoes. Sweeney testified that he couldn't absolutely match the shoes to the print, but the mark they made was consistent.

By August 20, just eight days after the trial began, the state rested its case against Gary Grant. The prosecution played the recording of Grant's statement to George Helland about the murder of Joanne Zulauf.

"What happened after you hit her?" the jury heard Helland ask Grant.

"She fell to her knees," Grant said. "I started going for her. She started to say something or scream. I grabbed her around the throat."

The defense began its case the next day. In their opening statements, the attorneys asked the jury to "view the defendant as the human being he is." Their only hope in the case was to convince the jury that Gary Grant was not sane when he committed the murders and to save him from the imposition of the death penalty.

Attorney Nick Marshall told the jury that Grant "suffers from a split personality. An unconscious rage existed in this man at the time of the murders.

"Testimony for the defense," he continued, "will show that Grant is normally very quiet and nonviolent and often experiences dreams and visions of grandeur."

He told the jury that Grant's earliest memories were of his parents fighting, with "extreme turmoil in his early years of life." He described Grant joining the navy, only to be sent home as a "mamma's boy," sending him back to the same turmoil from which he was trying to escape.

The first witness for the defense was Grant's close friend Frank Piggott. He testified about his relationship with Gary. "Gary was a quiet and easygoing guy who would go out of his way to help a person," Piggott testified.

"We'd go to the beach together or just hang out [at a Renton drive-in] or go to Safeway to watch people drive around the loop."

Piggott described a series of parties he and Grant had attended the previous September. It was at one of those parties that Grant gave his girlfriend a watch.

He talked about a time that month when, for the first time, he and Grant got into a fight over a girl. "That was the first time I saw him lose his temper," he told the jury. He said they'd patched things up that same night, and he didn't notice anything different about Grant's behavior.

It was the night before Joanne Zulauf was killed.

Glen Grant testified next. He told the jury that his son loved animals and was despondent when they died. He described Gary's home environment as "rough" due to his wife and her problems with alcohol and their constant quarreling. Mr. Grant described the separation he and Gary had to endure.

"My wife liked to throw things," he told the jury. "Pots and pans—whatever was convenient. Gary was home when most of that happened."

He described one particularly violent argument. "Gary started to cry. He said he couldn't take it anymore. We sent him to live with relatives in Oregon for about four months, but that wasn't a good environment."

He described Gary joining the navy, only to be sent home after about two months, allegedly witnessing "unnecessary brutality" on the part of a navy chief.

Mr. Grant, who had worked briefly as a Pierce County sheriff's deputy before working as a residential security guard, told the jurors that he had always taught Gary to cooperate with the police. He said he believed Renton detectives stalled him in his attempts to speak with Gary until they had a confession.

A psychiatrist testified about Grant's lack of mental awareness and his psychological disconnect from the facts of this case. If the jury were not to return the death penalty, he opined, Grant would likely be a model prisoner.

Though they had moved for a dismissal because of its existence, the defense inexplicably played for the jury the unlawfully recorded interview between Gary Grant and his first attorney, which had occurred at the Renton Police Department.

The defense's last witness in their case was Gary Grant himself.

"They put him on the stand," DiJulio said, "and he basically went into a trance. Marshall started questioning him, and once he got into the nitty-gritty, Nick just let him go. I don't remember if he admitted doing the murders, but he walked right up to them. You couldn't really cross-examine him, because he admitted it.

"We weren't completely sure he wasn't play-acting, but if he wasn't, it was a pretty good manner of doing it."

With that testimony, the defense rested.

In closing arguments, Edmund Allen asked the jury to find Grant guilty of all four murders and impose the death penalty for them. "The only real issue in the case is whether or not you impose the death penalty," Allen told the jury. "I

Gary Gene Grant

Gary Gene Grant was only twenty years old when he was charged with the four murders. *Courtesy of* Renton Record Chronicle.

Grant convicted; life is spared

By LARRY BROWN

A Superior Court jury today found Gary Gene Grant, 20, guilty of four counts of first-degree murder, but voted against imposing the death penalty.

The 10 men and two women had the case nearly 48 hours before returning the verdict to Judge David W. Soukup. They deliberated more than 18 hours.

Capital punishment was the principal issue in the case. Grant will be sentenced to up to life in prison.

Grant was accused in the slayings of Joanne Marie Zulauf, 17, by strangulation last September 20; Carole Adele Erickson, 19, by stabbing December 15, 1969; Bradley Lyons, 6, by strangulation last April 20, and Bradley's playmate, Scott Andrews, 6, by stabbing the same day.

Scott and Bradley were found slain in a wooded gulley inside the southeast city limit of Renton.

Miss Zulauf was found in

Gary Grant

a brushy area near Honey Creek, a half mile from her Renton home. She was un-

clad, but the medical examiner said she had not been assaulted sexually.

Miss Erickson, a foodservice employe at Renton Vocational School, was found slain near Airport Way and Logan Avenue North in Renton. She had been raped.

The case went to the jury Monday afternoon after seven days of testimony and argument.

The defense contended that Grant was "emotionally ill" at the time of the crimes. Grant gave statements admitting the slayings after he agreed to take a polygraph test relating to a knife found near where the boys were killed.

Grant was arrested after the knife was traced to him.

The prosecution told the jury that the case was "appropriate" for the death penalty.

The defense introduced testimony about "rough" conditions in the Grant home, and pleaded with the jury to consider Grant as "the human being he is."

The *Seattle Times* reported that Grant was convicted of four brutal murders. The jury, however, did not return the death penalty. *Courtesy of the* Seattle Times.

submit, though it is your decision, if ever an appropriate case for the death penalty exists, this is it."

Nick Marshall tried to convince the jury to see the human side of Gary Grant. "Try to put yourself in his shoes," he told them, "and look at him as a human being.

"Taking another life is not going to solve a thing. Nineteen years of misery, turmoil and hopelessness preceded the murders." He told them that Grant was "emotionally ill" at the time of the crimes. "He has a split personality," he continued, "marked by tender, loving care and unconscious rage."

After reading the jury instructions, Judge David Soukup adjourned for the day on August 23, 1971. The jury would begin deliberating the next morning.

On Wednesday, August 25, 1971, after two full days of deliberations, the jury returned a verdict: guilty of all four counts of murder. However, the jury did not impose the death penalty on Gary Grant.

With that, the work shifted to presentence reports and determining how long Grant would serve in prison.

Under the sentencing laws of that time, Grant could be sentenced to twenty years for murder in the first degree, which could be reduced to thirteen years, eight months with good behavior, if Judge Soukup decided the sentences for each murder should run concurrently; or the rest of

Grant's natural life, if he was given the maximum allowed punishment for each crime and they were run consecutively.

On September 29, 1971, Gary Grant appeared for sentencing before Judge David Soukup. Before Soukup handed down his sentence, the defense asked for a new trial. They said that the confession was illegal and was given under "coercion and duress" by Renton police. They also argued that there was a lack of evidence of premeditation and insisted that there should have been a separate trial for each murder and that they should have been able to introduce the confession to the crime by John Chance.

Judge Soukup denied the motions.

The prosecution asked for four consecutive life sentences with no possibility of parole. They cited a psychiatrist's presentence examination of Grant, in which he said Grant "at times doesn't know what he's doing" and could commit more murders.

Defense attorney Nick Marshall asked the court to impose concurrent terms, citing Grant's psychiatric problems and a different psychiatrist's opinion that he would be a model prisoner.

Judge Soukup followed the prosecution's recommendation, imposing four consecutive life terms, essentially sending Grant to prison for the rest of his natural life. Soukup acknowledged the defense's work in the case, telling them that he had no doubt they saved their client's life in persuading the jury not to sentence Grant to death.

Immediately after the sentencing, Marshall and co-counsel James Anderson withdrew as Grant's attorneys. Grant's parents had hired two different attorneys, James Grugg and Wesley Mohlbein, to appeal the conviction. The Grants were not pleased that Marshall and Anderson had not argued that Gary had not committed the murders at all. Grugg and Mohlbein said they would appeal the conviction based on the argument Marshall and Anderson made at sentencing, along with other issues.

The appeal was heard by a three-judge panel of the Washington Court of Appeals. On July 9, 1973, the appeals court returned its ruling on the appellate issues, finding no errors justifying dismissal of the charges or a new trial.

The defense requested a review by the Washington State Supreme Court. Its request was denied.

The team ultimately made a motion to appeal to the United States Supreme Court. On October 15, 1974, the U.S. Supreme Court denied the motion.

Grant's conviction and sentence would stand.

EPILOGUE

In her book *Through the Eyes of Serial Killers: Interviews with Seven Murderers* (Dundurn Press, 2015), Canadian author Nadia Fezzani printed letters she had exchanged with Gary Gene Grant for four years.

"There seemed to be little likelihood of finding Gary Grant. His name did not appear anywhere on the internet or in the works I had read," she said.

She described happening upon an article in the *Seattle Post-Intelligencer* written by my friend Levi Pulkkinen on serial killers from Washington State. The only information on Grant in that article was his number of victims, that he stabbed and/or strangled them and that they were dumped in the woods near his parents' home.

Grant, in his letters to Fezzani, claimed not to remember the crimes when he was arrested and asserted that's why he cooperated with Renton police at the beginning.

He related happy things early in his life. When she asked him about the more challenging aspects of his life, he wrote: "There are other memories which over time, I learned to lock away as if they never happened." He described being in his room, crying while his parents fought in other parts of the house, which he related to his mother's drinking.

Later, he described a "wrestling match" during which he lay in bed with his mother, naked.

He told Fezzani about being questioned about the knife. "They then told me that two six-year-old boys had been killed with that knife. I had no conscious memories of anything of that nature."

He recounted being taken to the Seattle Police Department to take a polygraph.

"I had nothing to hide," he said. "I wanted to prove I hadn't killed anyone."

He described the test. "I was taken into a room where a man was waiting with the lie detector on a table....In the beginning, he wanted me to lie in my answers to some of the questions so he could calibrate the machine. Then I was put through some psychiatric tests. It was the last memory I had of that day."

The next day, he was told he had confessed to all four murders and had written a confession, though he couldn't read and could barely write his own name. (The statement was written by Detective Hume based on the interview.)

"As you know, I was found guilty of all four murders and was sentenced to life in prison."

Thanks to counseling, he told Fezzani, he'd been able to externalize things he had locked away in his mind.

He told her of a night when he was home alone with his mother. She was cooking in the kitchen when he accidentally bumped into her. "She threatened me with her chopping knife. I ran to my bedroom and grabbed a fishing knife I had there with a fishing pole. As I came back out of my room, she came towards me in a fit of rage. I wanted to attack her, but the fear in me turned into that overwhelming fear I had of her, and I ran."

He described running down the railroad tracks armed with the knife. "Just then the girl walked past me. As she did so, that rage created by years and years of pain, fears, and frustrations, of anger and lust, came to the surface. This unknown girl became my mother and every girl who had ever laughed at me or made fun of me.

"Moving up behind her, I stabbed her in the back. Then I knelt down over her and choked her with my hands until she stopped moving."

Grant told Fezzani he undressed her with the intent to rape her, but memories of his mother made him run away.

Despite Grant denying raping Erickson, the autopsy showed she had indeed been raped. His exclusion of that is very telling. Grant compartmentalized his guilt in this crime, leaving out aggravating factors to make it more acceptable to him as a victim of his mother's undoubtedly actual abuse of him.

Grant described Zulauf's murder as also having occurred after an unpleasant experience with his mother. He then later described the Andrews and Lyons murders, telling Fezzani, "They became every boy who ever humiliated me."

To a jaded homicide detective like me, though Grant undoubtedly has deep-seated psychological issues, these seem like self-serving statements deflecting blame for these horrific crimes on someone else, implying it wasn't his fault.

A telling statement in Grant's writings to Fezzani is the statement, "In these times of rage, I lost all sense of right and wrong."

The very definition of legal insanity.

How convenient.

MANY OF THE PEOPLE associated with this crime died long ago.

John Chance, the mentally tortured man who at one time claimed to have killed Scott Andrews and Bradley Lyons, died in Tacoma in 1985.

CAPTAIN WILLIAM FRAZEE, WHO was responsible for the unlawful recording of Grant's conversations, particularly with his attorney, was forced to retire from the Renton Police Department. He pleaded guilty to the charge and was sentenced to four months' probation by Superior Court judge George R. Stuntz.

In sentencing Frazee, Stuntz noted his service as a police officer and acknowledged that Frazee had made a mistake out of his zeal to solve "one of the most brutal murders to ever occur in King County." Stuntz also ruled that the conviction be stricken from Frazee's record at the end of the probationary period.

After his career with the Renton police ended, Frazee went to work as a civilian warrant officer with the Seattle Police Department, arresting persons with outstanding misdemeanor warrants. Frazee died in May 1991. His obituary listed his friends' and family's discomfort in discussing what led to the end of his tenure in Renton.

THE SITES OF EACH of the crime scenes seem peaceful and quiet to those unaware of what happened there.

Carol Erickson's murder scene, just a mud-covered trail lined with scotch broom and other brush at the time of the murder, is now a well-maintained path along the river. A sculpture of a cat inadvertently sits at almost the same spot where her body was found that drizzly December morning in 1969.

The cabin where she lived and was walking to on the evening she was killed was long ago razed and is now the site of a latte stand. The old Kingen's Restaurant stands abandoned next door.

The trail where a neighbor saw Joanne Zulauf cut into the woods on a path—the last person to see her alive other than Gary Grant—has been developed. Houses sit on that spot today. The woods where her body was found are still there, quiet, peaceful and beautiful.

Shortly after her murder, her family left the area, moving to Idaho.

The place where the lives of two young and innocent boys, Scott Andrews and Bradley Lyons, were stolen is still a large wooded area overlooking the serenity of the Cedar River. Like all families of murdered children, the hole left in their parents' lives can never be filled.

This page, top: Carol Erickson's old address on Airport Way in Renton is now a latte stand. *Photo by Cloyd Steiger.*

This page, bottom: The site of Kingen's Restaurant is now vacant. Carol Erickson worked there the day she was murdered. *Photo by Cloyd Steiger.*

Opposite, top: The spot where Carol Erickson was found murdered is now a peaceful walkway. Few know of the horror that occurred there in 1969. *Photo by Cloyd Steiger.*

Opposite, bottom: Looking north from the Erickson scene today at the well-lit, paved promenade. *Photo by Cloyd Steiger.*

EPILOGUE

TO AN EXPERIENCED INVESTIGATOR, patterns are evident in all the murders:

All four victims were in wooded or isolated areas when the attacks occurred.

They were all blitz attacks with little or no interaction with the victims before the assaults.

Carol Erickson was stabbed and strangled; Joanne Zulauf was strangled; one of the boys was stabbed and the other strangled.

All were moved or dragged from the assault site to a nearby location.

All were partially or wholly disrobed and showed a possible sexual motivation.

All of the murders happened in relative proximity to the others.

LIKE IN ALMOST EVERY "whodunnit" murder, the case is fraught with rabbit holes that lure the detectives in, only to eventually be ruled out. The rabbit hole, in this case, was John Chance. Chance was the "too good to be true" suspect in the murders of Andrews and Lyons. He happened to show up at a nearby hospital talking about a desire to hurt children just when the boys were missing.

When detectives first interviewed Chance, he didn't seem to have any specifics about the crime. It wasn't until a couple of days later that he gave specific descriptions of how the scene looked.

When I reviewed old newspaper accounts of the crimes from just before Chance told detectives these facts, I found that they had all been released by Renton police to the press; Chance merely regurgitated what he had read in the papers. Circumstances such as this are precisely why (to the chagrin of many of my old friends in the media) it's imperative to hold back facts that only the real killer would know. That way, a detective speaking to the subject can see that what the person says isn't consistent with the scene. Both Jim Phelan and Wally Hume felt reticence about Chance as a suspect. They both said, "John Chance was a nut."

GARY GENE GRANT, SIXTY-EIGHT-YEAR-OLD prisoner number 127688, wiles away the hours in the Intensive Management Unit at the Washington State Penitentiary in Walla Walla, Washington, fifty years after the murder of Carol Erickson and forty-eight years after he was arrested. Even had the jury decided to impose the death penalty in his trial, the U.S. Supreme Court ruled the death penalty unconstitutional in 1973, converting everyone on death row around the country (including Charles Manson and his followers) to life sentences. That decision was later overturned.

The trailer park where Gary Grant lived a troubled life with his parents, near the shores of Lake Washington, was long ago removed. It was replaced with high-end condominiums after Coulon Park was built across Lake Washington Boulevard from the site.

The lives of the victims' families were forever ruined, and no prison sentence for Grant would change that. They were doomed to live with a hole in their hearts that could never be filled.

Carol Erickson should be in her late sixties, perhaps retired from a career as a chef, probably a mother and grandmother, enjoying time with her family.

Joanne Zulauf was only seventeen when her life was taken. Who knows where she would be if that hadn't happened? She also was deprived of the chance to live a long and happy life, get married, have children and build memories with them.

Scott Andrews and Bradley Lyons would be in their mid-fifties, probably thinking about retirement and what that would bring. Their two mothers likely dwell on the last time they saw the two boys, happy and playing as they walked toward the woods. If only they could go back and stop them.

Gary Grant sits in prison, an obscure and little-known serial killer. He has made claims that he doesn't remember the crimes.

The friends and families, police officers, detectives and prosecutors, as well as the people who lived in Renton during the time he sowed his savagery, will never forget him or what he did.

BIBLIOGRAPHY

Anderson, Robert D., MD. Psychiatric Evaluation of Gary Gene Grant. June 7, 1971.

Bayley, Christopher T. *Seattle Justice: The Rise and Fall of the Police Payoff System in Seattle.* Seattle, WA: Sasquatch Books, 2015.

Fezzani, Nadia. *Through the Eyes of Serial Killers: Interviews with Seven Murderers.* Toronto, CAN: Dundurn Publishing, 2015.

Harris, George Christian, MD. Psychiatric Evaluation of Gary Gene Grant. May 26, 1971.

Jarvis, Richard B., MD. Psychiatric Evaluation of John Arthur Chance. April 29, 1971.

Klein, Jack J., MD. Psychiatric Evaluation of John Arthur Chance. April 27, 1971.

Renton Historical Society and Museum Newsletter. "A Fiendish Deed Part I." March 2016.

———. "A Fiendish Deed Part II." June 2016.

Renton Record-Chronicle. "Arraignment of Murder Suspect Set Tomorrow." May 2, 1971.

———. "Base Camp Busy." April 23, 1971.

———. "Boys' Funerals Set for Tomorrow Morning." April 25, 1971.

———. "Concerned Parents Meet." May 7, 1971.

———. "Detectives Search Murder Scene." December 19, 1969.

———. "Double Murder Charges Filed." April 30, 1971.

———. "Eavesdropping Trial Date Set." May 21, 1971.

———. "Explorers Help in Search." September 23, 1970.

———. "Grant Had Poor School Record, Dropped Out." May 12, 1971.

———. "Grant Pleads Innocent to 4 Charges of Murder." May 19, 1971.

———. "Help Sought to Apprehend Killer; 2nd Girl Attacked." December 19, 1969.

———. "Man Linked to Four Renton Slayings." May 5, 1971.

———. "Missing Boys Found Dead in Remote Area." April 23, 1971.

———. "No Charges Filed against Witness in Slayings." May 9, 1971.

———. "No Leads Reported in Slaying." September 25, 1970.

———. "Official Portrait of 'Renton's Finest.'" December 18, 1968.

———. "Parents Unite to Help Fight Crime in Area." May 7, 1971.

———. "Police Call for Information about Slain Girl Brings Little Response." December 28, 1969.

———. "Police Captain Accused of Eavesdropping Given Leave." May 12, 1971.

———. "Police Not Talking about Man Being Held as Material Witness." May 7, 1971.

———. "Police Question Murder Suspect." April 25, 1971.

———. "Postponement in Arraignment of Frazee Granted." May 14, 1971.

———. "Quizzing of Slaying Suspect Continues." April 28, 1971.

———. "Renton Girl Found Slain." September 23, 1970.

———. "Renton Girl, 19, Murder Victim." December 17, 1969.

———. "Renton Police Chief Sees 'Good Case' against Grant." May 12, 1971.

———. "Renton's Grim Toll: 5 Murders in 2 Years." May 12, 1971.

———. "Safekeeping of Children Topic of Renton Parents." April 30, 1971.

———. "Tragedy." April 25, 1971.

———. "Youth Charged with 4 Murders." May 12, 1971.

Rule, Ann. *Empty Promises* (Ann Rules Crime Files Book 7). New York: Pocket Books, 2001.

Seattle Times. "Arrest of First Suspect in Slayings Ruled Reasonable." May 10, 1971.

———. "Closed Hearing Begins in Grant Murder Case." June 28, 1971.

———. "Explorers Look for Boys." April 22, 1971.

———. "4 Slayings: Gary Gene Grant Conviction Upheld." July 11, 1973.

———. "Girl, 19, Found Murdered in Renton." December 17, 1969.

———. "Grant Convicted." August 26, 1971.

———. "Grant Convicted; Life Is Spared." August 25, 1971.

———. "Grant Given Four Life Terms." September 29, 1971.

———. "Grant Murder Trial Put Off to Aug. 9." June 19, 1971.

————. "Hearing Set Monday in Grant Murder Case." June 23, 1971.

————. "Innocent Plea: Detective Denies Eavesdropping." May 20, 1971.

————. "Judge Denies Motions for Dismissal in Murder Case." July 1, 1971.

————. "Jury Ponders Death Penalty." August 24, 1971.

————. "Knife History Traced at Youth's Murder Trial." August 18, 1971.

————. "Knife Sought in Probe of 2 Slayings." April 27, 1971.

————. "Man Pleads Innocent in Boys Slayings." May 3, 1971.

————. "Murder Scene Is Described." August 17, 1971.

————. "Murder Suspect Was 'Bugged' Says Attorney." May 20, 1971.

————. Obituary of William Frazee. June 10, 1991.

————. "Officer Pleads Guilty of Aiding Illegal Recording." February 9, 1972.

————. "Police Continue to Question Suspect in Renton Slaying of Two Boys." April 24, 1971.

————. "Police Seek Clues on Slayer. Suspect Held." April 26, 1971.

————. "Police Seek Weapon in Slayings of Renton Boys." April 25, 1971.

————. "Police 'Snooping' Charged." May 10, 1971.

————. "Pretrial Hearing Begins in Slayings." August 3, 1971.

————. "Prosecution to Conclude Case in Murder Trial against Grant." August 20, 1971.

————. "Prosecution Using Watch to Link Murder Suspect." August 15, 1971.

————. "Renton Man Accused in Slayings." May 10, 1971.

————. "Renton Police Seek to Establish If Slain Girl Was at Library." December 19, 1969.

————. "Scout Team Looks for Boys." April 22, 1971.

————. "Tacoman Charged in Death of 2 Boys." April 29, 1971.

————. "Tacoman Charged in Death of 2 Boys." April 30, 1971.

————. "Testimony in Grant Trial Continues." August 16, 1971.

————. "3 Trials Sought for Grant." August 4, 1971.

————. "2 Deputy Prosecutors Resign County Posts." May 30, 1971.

————. "Young Man on Trial in Four Slayings." August 13, 1971.

————. "Youth's Trial Set July 6 in Four Renton Murders." May 11, 1970.

Stone, Arthur (Ann Rule). "Who Killed and Stabbed Carol Adele?" *Master Detective Magazine* 81, no. 3 (December 1970): 36.

Washington v. Gary Gene Grant. King County Superior Court case file. Cause #071056946, including police reports from the Renton Police Department and the King County Department of Public Safety.

Wikipedia. "Boeing Renton Factory." en.wikipedia.org/wiki/Boeing_Renton_Factory.

————. "Renton, Washington." en.wikipedia.org/wiki/Renton,_Washington.

INDEX

ABOUT THE AUTHOR

Cloyd Steiger was a homicide detective with the Seattle Police Department for the last twenty-two years of his thirty-six-year career. During that time, he investigated some of the most notorious murders in Seattle, including serial killers, mass murders, domestic terrorism resulting in death and just a lot of murders where one person kills another for no damned good reason.

He currently works as the chief criminal investigator for the Washington State Attorney General's Homicide Investigations Tracking System (HITS), where murder investigations are tracked in Washington, Oregon and Montana. HITS also helps agencies by suggesting investigative techniques in new and cold-case murders.

He is a consulting committee member of the American Investigative Society of Cold Cases (AISOCC), a national nonprofit that helps police agencies nationwide with the investigation of cold-case murders.

He is the author of *Homicide: The View from Inside the Yellow Tape—A True Crime Memoir.* He also writes a quarterly column, "Inside the Yellow Tape," for *Forensic Magazine.*

He is the father of three sons (two of whom are Seattle police officers) and six grandchildren. He lives in the Seattle area with his wife, Doreen, and killer Lhasa Apso Libby.